'Lymphoedema is a little-known illness and this book will help sufferers and their carers cope – and who better to help write it than someone like Gemma Levine who is a sufferer herself.'

– Dame Judi Dench

'I was always aware of the terrible disease lymphoma, as my dad died with that condition, but was totally unaware of the further ongoing condition lymphoedema. Any knowledge that can help explain this condition is a must-read.'

– Sir Alex Ferguson

'What we know about, we can work to heal, and in the meantime give strength to those who suffer. That is why this book is so important. I salute two remarkable people, Gemma Levine and Professor Peter Mortimer, for helping us learn about this terrible condition. Bless you both for opening our eyes and hearts.'

– Rabbi Lord Jonathan Sacks

'Cancer touches all our lives and it is a sad fact that lymphoedema affects 40 per cent of cancer patients. This condition has been widely ignored in our generation. Let us hope there will be a cure in our children's lifetime.'

– Dame Joan Collins

'It is important, when an unfamiliar condition with a strange name is explained, for us all to understand. That is what is happening here. As a result, those who have suffered in the shadows will now know their condition is widely recognised and th⸍⸍ sympathy and concern.'

'At last someone has written something about this debilitating condition, which causes so much suffering; this is a book that needed to be written and should be read.'

– Lord Paddy Ashdown

'This is exactly what people suffering from lymphoedema need to have by them; professionally informed, but with the insight of those who live with it on a day-to-day basis.'

– Lord David Owen

'Lymphoedema is the ugly child of cancers which, although widespread, is largely unknown. Peter Mortimer and Gemma Levine have brought it into the light where, I hope, it can be exposed and defeated.'

– Sir John Major

'Professor Mortimer, one of the very top specialists of this debilitating condition, and Gemma Levine, a brave and determined sufferer and photographer, have come together to give help and support to others with this affliction.'

– Olga and Alex Polizzi

'This subject is worthy of a dedicated book. It's time for help and comfort to be shared and given, by true professionals, in this powerful publication. It is not soon enough.'

– Baroness Betty Boothroyd

'Such understanding and openness offer the hope not just of better treatment, but ultimately of a cure for a hidden disease that affects too many.'

– Lord Michael Dobbs

'This book clearly explains this little-understood condition and focuses our attention on ways to support those who live with it.'

– Angela Rippon

'A ghastly condition, too widely ignored. I hate to think how it affects Gemma, a lifelong photographer who is now unable to lift a camera – which was second nature to her existence.'

– Joanna Lumley

'This book will help to shed light on a distressing and debilitating condition.'

– Jack Dee

'So many of our colleagues in the world of music rely on hand and arm movements to play their instruments. With lymphoedema, it is impossible. It is incredibly depressing to know that there are those who have had to drop out of the profession for this reason. We hope one day there will be a cure.'

– Sir Karl and Lady Jenkins

'It is appalling to know that lymphoedema can be caused by efforts to get rid of cancer. Yet another challenge for the medical profession, and I applaud books like this for bringing it out from the shadows.'

– John Suchet

'Had I had the horrifying misfortune of lymphoedema in my hands, I would not have been able to butter bread, never mind cook for the glitterati and end up with a Michelin star. People with this terrible affliction deserve our support.'

– Prue Leith

'It is wonderful that there have been significant advances in treating lymphoedema as a result of the work of Professor Peter Mortimer. But equally important is the perspective of sufferers like Gemma Levine to help those who are having to cope with this affliction.'

– Lord Richard Harries

'I hope this book will bring help and relief to the many sufferers of lymphoedema, while also enlightening those of us who know so little about it.'

– Sir Stirling Moss

'This is an obscure but terrible affliction. This book fills a huge gap in our knowledge.'

– Frederick Forsyth

'Professor Mortimer and Gemma Levine are to be congratulated on bringing understanding of this little-known condition to a wider public.'

– Terry Waite

'*Let's Talk Lymphoedema* is of utmost importance in making us all aware of this terrible condition and how to cope with it.'

– Nicole Farhi

'This is a vitally important book about a dreadful condition that affects so many people but receives so little attention.'

– Piers Morgan

Let's Talk Lymphoedema

THE ESSENTIAL GUIDE
TO EVERYTHING
YOU NEED TO KNOW

Professor Peter Mortimer
& Gemma Levine

First published 2017 by
Elliott and Thompson Limited
27 John Street, London WC1N 2BX
www.eandtbooks.com

ISBN: 978-1-78396-285-3

Text © Peter Mortimer 2017
Photographs © Gemma Levine 2017
Copyright in the contributions © the Contributors 2017

9 8 7 6 5 4 3 2 1

A catalogue record for this book is available from the British Library.

Design: Karin Fremer
Typesetting: Servis Film Setting

Printed in the UK by TJ International Ltd

Contents

Foreword   ix

What Is the Purpose of this Book?   xi

Preface   xiii

Introduction by Gemma Levine   1

1. Introducing the Lymph System   5

2. What Is Lymphoedema?   11

3. The Perils of Infection   17

4. What Causes Lymphoedema?   25

5. How Common Is Lymphoedema?   41

6. Awareness and Diagnosis   47

7. Standard Treatments   69

8. New and Alternative Treatments   101

9. Managing Obesity and Lymphoedema   115

10. Living with Lymphoedema   123

11. Children with Lymphoedema   145

12. Other Forms of Lymphoedema   159

13. Lymphoedema Worldwide   175

     Conclusion: Hope   187

     Appendix 1: Exercises   189

     Appendix 2: Nutrition   197

     Resources   200

     Acknowledgements   201

     Index   204

Foreword

This book, the first of its kind, addresses the underestimated healthcare problem of lymphoedema, through patient stories from throughout the world. In the UK, if it is known about at all, it is usually through its association with breast cancer, although there are many other causes.

As President of Sightsavers, an international non-governmental organisation that works with partners in developing countries to treat and prevent avoidable blindness, I have taken an interest in the progress towards the elimination of neglected tropical diseases, of which lymphoedema is one.

I am pleased to see that a neglected tropical disease features in this book. What is not realised is that lymphoedema causes similar suffering in our own communities and is equally overlooked.

My hope is that this book will bring much needed attention to this neglected condition.

HRH Princess Alexandra

What Is the Purpose of this Book?

Do your feet and ankles tend to swell up on long-haul flights or in the heat? Do you occasionally suffer from prolonged and sometimes severe swelling in one foot? In fact, do you ever experience swelling in the arm, leg, or any part of the body? If so, there is a chance that you have lymphoedema. And the chances are that – like the vast majority of sufferers – you are not aware of having the condition, and probably haven't even heard of it.

Lymphoedema is a hidden epidemic. It is one of the least recognised illnesses – among both doctors *and* patients. Those who have heard of of lymphoedema tend to associate it with arm swelling after breast cancer treatment. However, there are many causes: there are genetically based forms, which may be present from a young age; in tropical countries it is most commonly associated with filariasis, a mosquito-borne disease; and in the Western world the increase in obesity is now also making the condition more widespread.

There is no cure but effective treatments do exist to alleviate symptoms so that lymphoedema can be well managed and sufferers can live a full and active life.

The aim of this book is to give ordinary people, their friends, relatives, carers and doctors the information and insight needed to understand lymphoedema fully. It does so by shining a light on this neglected condition, explaining in simple terms and with carefully chosen images what it is, how it is caused, how it affects sufferers, how it is diagnosed and how its symptoms can be managed. It includes contributions from experts in the field, but also from patients themselves (all patient names have been changed) – in the UK, USA, India and Ethiopia – so that it offers a view of lymphoedema that is at once informed, global and personal.

We hope it will help raise awareness and understanding of the condition, and improve the lives of sufferers as much as possible.

Preface

When Gemma approached me to help her write a book on lymphoedema, I was immediately excited. Here was a famous photographer, with hugely influential connections and contacts, who had already written the bestseller *Go with the Flow* on her experience of breast cancer. I have specialised in the diagnosis and treatment of lymphoedema for over thirty years and it is a constant battle to get more public recognition of the problem. This was a fantastic – and timely – opportunity.

When I started my training at the John Radcliffe Hospital in Oxford in 1981 my boss, Professor Terence Ryan, sat me down and suggested I do some research. He said that if I specialised in lymphoedema I would be a world expert in two years. At the time I was flattered, thinking he was commenting on my ability and potential, but I soon realised that it was nothing to do with me. What he was really saying was that if you are the only one studying something it is not difficult to become the expert on it. It was a sadly accurate reflection of how neglected lymphoedema has always been. As renowned medical researcher Philip McMaster said in his William Harvey Lecture of 1942: 'The functions of the lymphatic system have remained largely unknown [since its discovery]. Two influences have contributed to our state of ignorance, a lack of suitable methods of study . . . and a lack of interest.'

That sentiment has remained much the case to this day but

now interest in lymphatic science is growing fast. The discovery of genes causing lymphoedema has increased our understanding of how the condition can develop, and I predict that, in the foreseeable future, new treatments will become available. In the meantime we need to do all we can to raise awareness of this condition, which can cause huge physical and psychological suffering, and make sure that healthcare professionals are taking notice and doing all they can to help their patients. That is why I agreed so readily to work with Gemma on this book, which I hope will help put an end to all these many years of neglect.

Professor Peter Mortimer

Introduction by Gemma Levine

A few years ago I was diagnosed with breast cancer and had surgery to remove a tumour from my right breast and a mastectomy. Shortly after going through the trauma of chemotherapy and radiotherapy, I discovered my arm was grossly swollen and reddish, and it felt heavy and painful. I visited my surgeon who said, 'You have lymphoedema, that's very unlucky.'

I did not know what lymphoedema was – I hadn't even heard of it before. The nurse thrust a small booklet into my hand and suggested I had a few sessions with a remedial massage specialist. Innocently I thought a series of six visits would cover it. It didn't. I have since learnt it will last my lifetime.

The onset of lymphoedema was gradual for me. My arm became heavy and thick, my skin became soft and pitted and my movements increasingly restricted. I can no longer use my right hand to carry parcels, lift items from high shelves, remove hot dishes from an oven, use scissors or handle large bars of soap when showering. I can only wash my hair with my strong arm, and I cannot wear T-shirts or other close-fitting garments. I was advised not to travel on long flights, so I limit myself to a maximum of two to three hours and I have to keep my arm elevated, otherwise it becomes excessively heavy. But most important is the effect it has had on my lifelong profession as a portrait photographer. I can no longer hold heavy cameras. Recently I was fortunate to be able to purchase an Apple iPad, which is light and easy to handle. I was astonished that I could achieve the same results with an iPad, or even iPhone, as with my professional cameras. So I am able to continue to explore my creativity and still experience the joy and fulfilment of my profession.

To maintain my quality of life I have to be disciplined with my exercise and new regime. I swim every morning and have devised a routine exercise programme (which is at the end of this book). I visit a lymphoedema specialist, Carmel Phelan, once a month, who keeps a measurement check on my arm, administers manual lymphatic drainage and changes my compression garments if needed. I also use a machine that was sent to me from the USA, a 'Bio Compression' pump, which moves up and down the arm gently and rhythmically.

A year ago, I took part in a BBC2 documentary during which I was filmed in my home. During the interview my local GP, Dr Nazeer, came to visit. I was wearing my compression sleeve as he examined my arm and asked how my lymphoedema was responding to self-management. The whole clip lasted no more than two minutes. Some months later, on the night it was broadcast, I checked my emails at the end of the programme and discovered, to my utter surprise, there were around forty in my inbox. A few were from friends and family, commenting on the programme, but the others were from people around the country asking questions about my condition or commenting on how rare it was to see it featured on TV. Yvette from the Midlands said, 'Lymphoedema awareness is so not out there . . . It is a restricted condition with misunderstood information, sadly with a growing audience out there too.' Shaemus from Ireland wrote that, 'Lymphoedema is the poor relation to cancer in respect of media attention.'

This reaction to the documentary was a wake-up call for me. Ah! I thought. There's a need here for a serious book. I started to do some research and then, armed with my newfound facts, I visited my oncologist, Professor Paul Ellis, who put me in touch with his colleague Peter Mortimer, Professor of Dermatological Medicine at St George's and the Royal Marsden Hospitals, internationally known for his expertise in lymphoedema. When I eventually met him, we discussed the concept of a book and agreed to combine our efforts. With his exceptional knowledge of the condition, there could be nobody better to collaborate with, to move the project forward in the right direction. A few weeks later we had a plan.

Since then, I have learnt and seen so much of the stages of the condition and the various types affecting men, women and children, not all of which are related to cancer, as mine is. I have also been surprised by the number of people I've encountered who are familiar with lymphoedema. Kristina, my friend from Finland, told me her mother had developed lymphoedema in 1963 at the age of forty-eight, in the same arm as myself. She had no real regular physiotherapy, just instructions to massage herself daily. 'She wore a bind around the arm, a sort of stretchy bandage from armpit to wrist. It was quite an effort, as she had no strength in the arm.' And once, while in a restaurant in Venice, a waiter eyed up my compression sleeve and asked, 'What is the matter with your arm?' I replied 'You won't know what this is, it's called lymphoedema.' 'Oh!' he exclaimed. 'Yes I do, it's a reminder of a cancer operation you had, where you have been lucky enough to survive. What a meaningful reminder.'

More recently, I was in Waitrose, Oxford Street and when I asked for home-delivery, which I am reliant on as I cannot carry the bags, I was told the driver was away sick. The manager, Annette, took the bags and said she would assist me to the street and put me in a cab. On our way up the escalator, she asked what was wrong with my arm. I said, yet again, 'You won't know what this is, it's called lymphoedema.' 'Yes I do,' she said, and tears filled her eyes. 'My best friend has just been told she has it and is in tremendous discomfort and doesn't know what to do.' When I told her that I was about to publish a book on the subject, she said, 'With the very little knowledge there is today of the condition, it will be one of the most valuable books and will help thousands of people.' With that, she put her arms around me, hugged me and we parted.

The physical, emotional and psychological effects of lymphoedema cannot be underestimated. From my experience it is essential that we have specialist consultants and practitioners to provide sufferers with the knowledge, advice and vital treatment that they need to cope with this condition.

Let's Talk Lymphoedema is exactly what this book is all about. It is our aim to inform sufferers, friends and family of its debilitating and lifelong effects, and to help them deal with those effects. I am profoundly privileged and proud, to have collaborated with the experts in this country and worldwide who have contributed to this publication, but in particular, Professor Peter Mortimer who has devoted time and expertise to advancing this cause, which has been his lifelong endeavour. I have also photographed many patients: symbolic photographs that illustrate the workings of the lymphatic system; a micro-surgery unit within a hospital; preparing bandaging and lymphatic drainage treatments; a compression garment factory in Germany and many more.

I hope this book will be a powerful tool in the struggle to raise awareness of lymphoedema. It includes the most up-to-date information and advice from around the world, and has a powerful message for sufferers: that they are not alone or forgotten, and that they can still lead rich and vibrant lives.

Gemma Levine

1

Introducing the Lymph System

'I had little idea what the lymph system was until my (best) friend Ross got lymphoma, which is a cancer of the lymph system. I now know how important the lymph system is for keeping us healthy and how important exercise and, particularly, sport are for it to function properly.'

Sir Andy Murray (twice Wimbledon champion, US Open tennis champion, twice Olympic singles champion, Davis Cup winner for GB)

This book is not about cancer, but it is about the lymph system, a part of our body most people know very little about, and one of the problems that arises when it does not work properly: lymphoedema. To understand the condition fully, we need to first understand a little bit about the lymph system and how it works.

WHAT IS THE LYMPH SYSTEM?

Most of us are familiar with the idea that the heart circulates blood around the body, carrying the oxygen, nutrients and fluid that all the different types of cell in our bodies need to work. This is called our cardiovascular system and it operates along a network of blood vessels such as arteries, capillaries and veins.

What most of us don't realise is that we also have a second circulatory system called the lymph system. It acts as the drainage route for the body's cells, carrying away excess fluid, waste materials, immune cells and proteins from the tissues. The fluid that leaves the cells and enters the lymph system is called lymph, and the system itself is made up a network of lymph vessels and glands (which are sometime referred to as 'nodes').

HOW DOES THE LYMPH SYSTEM WORK AND WHY IS IT IMPORTANT?

The way that lymph moves through the body is a little bit like the way rainwater makes its way to the sea. When it rains, drops of water drain through the soil and then enter rivulets and streams. These in turn flow in a one-way direction, joining bigger and bigger river channels until finally they empty out into the sea.

Lymph flows in much the same way. It drains from individual body cells into the smallest lymph vessels, which are much like the tentacles on sea anemones. Lymph then travels in a one-way direction through a network of increasingly bigger lymph vessels until it eventually completes its journey in the upper chest where it discharges into two big veins. The lymph fluid, now mixed back into the bloodstream, will then either flow back out to the tissues or, if there is excess fluid in the body, it will be excreted through the kidneys and exit the body through the bladder. The lymph system is therefore instrumental in controlling the amount of fluid in the entire body, i.e. both in the tissues and the blood.

As it moves along the lymph system, the lymph fluid itself passes through a series of lymph glands. There are hundreds of glands in the human body, each one the size of a small bean. They are situated in varying numbers around the body, but tend to cluster near major junctions in the lymph system, in areas such as the neck, armpit and groin.

The smallest lymph vessels, which absorb fluid from the tissues, are tubes that resemble the tentacles on sea anemones.

Lymph glands perform two basic functions: they clean up the lymph before it re-enters the bloodstream, by sieving out, trapping and destroying foreign materials; and they monitor the lymph for telltale signs of infection in the body, playing a vital role in our immune system.

Immune cells are released from blood vessels throughout the body in order to patrol the tissues looking for germs. If they encounter the germs that cause infection, such as bacteria, viruses and fungi, the immune cells exit the tissues via the lymph vessels and head for the lymph glands. Once there they trigger an immune response, whereby the lymph glands produce and mobilise other immune cells specifically tailored to kill the offending germs. These immune cells then travel from the lymph glands along the lymph system, into the blood stream and back to the site of infection to kill the germs.

HOW DOES LYMPH FLOW?

The flow of the lymph system is vital to its healthy operation. Blood is pumped through the body by the heart. The lymph system, on the other hand, requires movement and exercise to make lymph flow. If we do not move much, neither does the lymph.

The movements we make during our everyday activities involve the expansion and contraction of the various muscles in our bodies. These muscle movements in turn serve to massage and squeeze the tissues around them, forcing excess fluid out of the tissues and into the smallest lymph vessels. The same principle also drives lymph along the tiny lymph vessel tubes and keeps the process going: when the muscles relax and the 'squeeze' stops, the tissues recoil, so allowing the now empty lymph vessels to suck up more fluid from the tissues.

The process is similar to what happens when you squeeze and release a sponge underwater. Squeezing a wet sponge drives water out through the pores and from the network of channels within the sponge. Releasing the sponge under water then absorbs water back into the sponge where it stays until the sponge is next squeezed.

The larger lymph vessels further along the lymph system have special muscle cells built into their walls. This allows the vessels to generate their own contractions, propelling the lymph onwards – up a leg or an arm, for example. These larger vessels are split into segments separated by one-way valves – so that they look much like a string of sausages. As one section contracts, the lymph is pumped through the open valve into the next section, with the valve preventing reverse flow so that the lymph always moves in one direction, much like lock gates on a canal, which ensure the water can only flow one way.

The valves within lymph vessels work like canal lock gates, ensuring lymph can only flow in one direction.

HOW DOES THIS RELATE TO LYMPHOEDEMA?

Lymphoedema occurs when the lymph system fails: lymph vessels can get blocked or close down at some point along the drainage route; valves can fail allowing the lymph to flow backwards, towards the tissues; and the ability of the lymph vessels to contract can fail, in which case lymph is not pumped towards and beyond the glands.

Any impairment to the lymph drainage system causes the fluid to back up and collect within the tissues instead of draining away. As we will see in the next chapter, one of the most immediate and obvious symptoms of lymphoedema is therefore swelling, but there are many more potential symptoms and complications.

2

What Is Lymphoedema?

Lymphoedema is a chronic condition caused by a failure in the lymph system, meaning lymph is not draining from the body. There are many reasons why it might fail (see Chapter 4) but the end result is generally the same: a build-up of fluid in the tissues causing chronic swelling with thickened skin.

WHERE DOES LYMPHOEDEMA OCCUR?

The build-up of fluid associated with lymphoedema can occur anywhere where there is impaired flow in the lymph system – whether in the smallest lymph vessels, the larger vessels or, most commonly, in the various lymph glands located around the system. For example, a problem with the lymph glands in the left armpit could lead to lymphoedema occurring anywhere 'up river' from that point – i.e. the left breast, the upper left-hand side of the trunk, and the whole of the left arm. Similarly, if there is an impairment to the lymph glands in your right groin area, this could lead to problems in the adjoining side of the lower abdomen below the belly button, or anywhere along your right leg. In this case, due to the influence of gravity, you would be most likely to experience swelling in the foot, ankle and lower leg.

Lymphoedema most commonly occurs in the arm or leg, but it can appear in other parts of the body as well. It is less likely, however, to appear in the genitalia or in the head and neck area. This is because these areas of the body have lymph drainage on both sides, so there would have to be a problem on both sides to cause lymphoedema to occur.

It is worth re-emphasising that lymphoedema is not always caused by problems in the lymph glands – if there is sufficient compromise in lymph flow at any point along the drainage pathway then swelling can occur. For example, lymphoedema of the foot could result from impaired drainage within the small lymph capillaries of the foot; from a failure of the main lymph vessels of the leg to pump properly; or from obstruction in the groin.

FLUID RETENTION AND SWELLING

Lymphoedema literally means 'swelling caused by the build-up of lymph fluid'. It can develop in different ways, but generally starts as mild, reversible swelling, that may go away at first, but at some point will become more permanent. It often becomes particularly noticeable when lymph drainage is put under stress – for example, during an extended period of inactivity such as on a long-haul flight. In practice this swelling might mean that the rings on your fingers start to feel tight, your face and tummy become bloated, or your ankles begin to balloon. This swelling can then in turn cause further symptoms such as heaviness, aching and a general discomfort.

One problem with diagnosing lymphoedema (see Chapter 6) is that it shares many characteristics with 'oedema', which is a swelling caused by the retention of any fluid. Oedema can often occur during pregnancy, before a period or sometimes in the heat (due to a redistribution of fluid). However, it can also be a sign of a serious medical condition such as heart, kidney or liver disease, so it is important that a complete assessment is carried out to exclude these possibilities.

In fact, to make diagnosis more complicated, all cases of oedema involve the lymph system because oedema occurs when blood vessels under the skin release more fluid into the tissues than the lymph vessels can drain away. The difference between oedema and lymphoedema is that oedema affects the lymph system, whereas lymphoedema is caused by a fault in the lymph system and involves a build-up of lymph rather than just fluid.

Since lymph contains other elements including waste products and immune cells, the swelling produced by lymphoedema tends to have a more solid texture to it. The fluid in oedema, on the other hand, can be displaced by pressure, and so indents, or pits, very easily if a finger is pressed on the skin. A good example of pitting is the indentation left by pressure from the rim of a sock. This can be tested to some extent by pressing a fingertip firmly on the skin surface for twenty seconds (assuming it is not painful). If a dent from your finger remains after release, then you have fluid oedema.

THICKENING SKIN

Over time lymphoedema can cause changes to take place in the skin, making it much thicker. The worse the swelling, and the longer lymphoedema has been allowed to progress, the worse the skin becomes – it can often become twice as thick as it would normally be. We don't know why this happens, but it is probably a response to the pressure of the fluid collection within the skin, as well as the effect of inflammation from the disturbed immune cells.

The surface of the skin can also develop a warty complexion and can start to look like the bark of a tree or elephant hide. The term

In longstanding lymphoedema the skin can become so thick that it can look and feel like the bark on a tree.

'elephantiasis', which is sometimes used instead of lymphoedema, comes from this change in complexion of the skin and the fact that the swollen leg could be said to resemble that of an elephant.

OTHER HEALTH FACTORS AND SYMPTOMS

Although swelling is the main symptom associated with lymphoedema, it's not the only health problem sufferers can experience. Because the lymph system is responsible for removing virtually all excess and waste products from the body's tissues, if it is not working properly, it can affect other aspects of our health. One example is cardiovascular disease, which arises when the walls of the arteries become 'furred up' by cholesterol deposits. There is some evidence to suggest that these deposits can partly be explained by a failure of lymph drainage within the cells of the arterial walls.

The lymph system is also important for maintaining a healthy body fluid balance, which means that any impairment could possibly contribute to raised blood pressure. There is also a strong association between lymphoedema and obesity (see Chapter 4) and this association is known to work in both directions: obesity is the biggest risk factor for lymphoedema but lymphoedema can also cause obesity. However, as we shall discuss in the next chapter, the main problem associated with lymphoedema is infection – particularly cellulitis, which can pose a serious health risk.

3

The Perils of Infection

The lymph system plays an important part in our immune system (see Chapter 1), so any impairment to the lymph system can lead to problems with infection.

We come into contact with germs all the time. More often than not, our immune system – with our lymph system in support – deals with these germs without us knowing about it. Sometimes we may be aware of slightly enlarged lymph glands from a sore throat – an indication that the body is fighting infection – but otherwise we are not ill. On other occasions we feel unwell and feverish with aching and headache, which are signs the immune system has had to go into overdrive to fight the infection.

With lymphoedema, the failure of the lymph system means that the immune system is compromised, and can't fight infection. It doesn't affect the entire body (unlike HIV, which is the disease that usually comes to mind when we think of a compromised immune system) – it just affects the area where the lymphoedema is present. However, that area becomes very susceptible to infections, which are difficult to eradicate and can keep coming back. A recent UK study showed that infection was common among lymphoedema sufferers, with 60 per cent having experienced at least one episode during the previous six months, and 22 per cent of those having been admitted to hospital for treatment of the infection.

'I had lymphoedema in my right leg
for a few weeks after a major operation
for bladder cancer some years ago. I
was lucky in that it resolved, but many
cancer survivors are not so fortunate.
This book will be of great help to them
in understanding and self-managing
this distressing condition'

Dame Mary Archer

CELLULITIS

One type of infection that is especially associated with lymphoe-dema is cellulitis – a painful and potentially serious infection of the skin, which often leads to septicaemia, or blood poisoning. It can cause profound illness with high temperatures and low blood pressure, with the accompanying threat of damage to vital organs. In Europe it is also known as erysipelas, and in the tropics it can be called acute dermato-lymphangio-adenitis (ADLA) when associated with elephantiasis.

Cellulitis is most often caused by some form of surface skin break – a cut or insect bite for example – that introduces bacteria into the region, where the immune system is unable to deal with it. This is one of the reasons skin care is so important in managing lymphoedema (see page 95), although there are other ways the harmful bacteria can enter the body.

RECURRING INFECTIONS

People who suffer with lymphoedema often find that infections, such as cellulitis, can easily recur; in some cases striking as soon as you have recovered from the previous bout. It remains unproven but it is more than likely that in some cases, because of the weakened immune system, the infection is never properly eradicated. Antibiotics used to treat infection are intended to aid your immune system, so if your immune response is impaired, they are not always effective. This would explain why some patients with lymphoedema and recurrent cellulitis find that they can bring on an attack just by getting overtired, overstressed or by over-exercising. As one patient explained: 'It's as if the infection is asleep in my leg all the time and then, when it sees I am run down, it wakes up to take advantage.'

Recurrent attacks of cellulitis can be one of the most distressing and frightening aspects of having lymphoedema. Attacks can come on without warning, sometimes mild, sometimes severe, with no rhyme or reason as to why one attack might be more debilitating than another. This element of unpredictability can be extremely unsettling and discourages people from making plans for holidays or long-distance travel in case infection strikes.

A UK government report in 2009 stated that cellulitis was among the top ten reasons for admission to hospital, accounting for over 45,000 emergency admissions per year. A significant proportion of those patients will have lymphoedema, but many may not yet have a diagnosis. Unfortunately, in most cases, staff haven't been trained to recognise that more than one attack of cellulitis in the same area always indicates underlying lymphoedema, as James discovered when he started suffering from recurrent infections:

James is fifty-five and works for an airline, which often means having to fly every two weeks or so. He had noticed that his ankles would swell on flights; the longer the flight the worse the swelling. Heat would also make the swelling worse. He knew it was fluid because he could make an indentation by pressing his thumb into his shin. The swelling did not hurt, and if he elevated his legs and wore flight socks on trips, he could just about control it. Then, around Christmas two years ago, he suddenly became unwell with high fever. He was shivery, had a headache and felt sick. He thought he had the flu but then realised his right leg was painful, bright red and hot to the touch. He immediately went to hospital where he was admitted with cellulitis.

After five days on a drip having intravenous antibiotics and then a further two-week course of antibiotics he made a full recovery. The leg oedema was much the same as it had been before so he carried on as usual. Then nine months later he had a further attack of cellulitis. He recognised the symptoms, so he went to his GP who prescribed antibiotics. Although he did not feel as ill as he had during the first attack and did not have to spend time in hospital, he was forced to take three weeks off work.

Five months later he became very unwell and collapsed. He was rushed to hospital by ambulance and admitted immediately. Cellulitis of the same right leg was diagnosed again. After ten days on a drip he was allowed home on oral antibiotics but remained concerned that the leg still hurt and was red. Returning to work a month later, he almost immediately suffered another attack of cellulitis, the fourth, in the same leg.

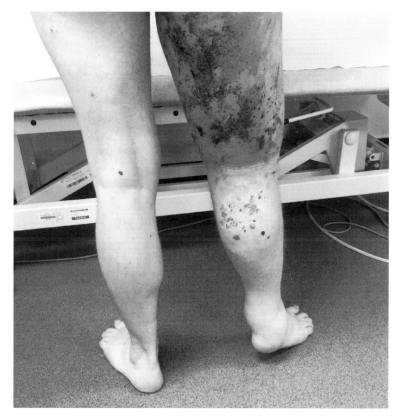

Lymphoedema in a young man due to a genetic fault in the formation of the lymph vessels within the leg from birth. Multiple, repeat infections have resulted in further damage to lymph vessels and severe staining of the skin.

James's case shows us that when a patient has lymphoedema it is difficult to eradicate infection. Furthermore, without diagnosing the condition and addressing the underlying lymph drainage problem, the swelling and infection will only get worse: the greater the swelling the more likely it is that an infection will take hold, and every episode of infection can cause further damage to lymph vessels, so making the lymphoedema worse. It is a vicious circle.

Another important point to make is that it is not normal to experience swelling so severe that you have to make adjustments in your life, such as James did when wearing flight socks and keeping his foot elevated. Persistent or recurrent swelling in the feet, ankles or legs suggests a lymph problem, and should be checked out.

However, even when the underlying cause has been diagnosed as lymphoedema, that doesn't necessarily help when dealing with the infections, as Sarah found out:

Sarah was only thirty-two years old when she developed lymphoedema following treatment for cancer of the cervix. The lymphoedema affected not only both of her legs but also the lower abdomen and external genitalia. The pressure of the lymph fluid within the skin of the genitals led to small blisters which would then leak lymph, making her feel as if she had wet herself.

Not long after developing lymphoedema, she started to suffer from bouts of cellulitis. The severity of the attacks would vary but she frequently had to be admitted to hospital to be treated for septicaemia. Then the attacks started to become more frequent. She was prescribed continuous antibiotics but even that did not stop them. Her swelling got worse as did the leaking of lymph fluid, and her overall health deteriorated, both physically and psychologically. She was always tired, even between infections. She was a police officer but gradually became unable to stay on her feet all day or chase criminals on the street. Sadly she was forced into early retirement on medical grounds from a job she loved at the age of forty-five. After that, the attacks of cellulitis were not as frequent or severe, but they still did not stop altogether. Her legs remained huge and heavy, making it difficult to walk any distance or find clothes to fit.

At forty-nine she was given the go-ahead to have liposuction treatment on the NHS, which not only reduced the
size of her legs but, for reasons not fully understood, also
led to less frequent attacks of cellulitis and she no longer
needed continuous antibiotics.

Despite Sarah receiving excellent care, the vicious cycle of relentless swelling and attacks of infection could not be broken. Because
she had one huge leg, and most of the swelling was found to be fat
related to the lymphoedema, she was funded to have liposuction
to reduce its size. This did not cure her lymphoedema and she still
had to wear compression garments night and day to control the
remaining fluid, but the relentless recurrent attacks of cellulitis
finally ceased, also ending her fear of them, and her quality of life
improved enormously. It's not known exactly why liposuction can
end the cycle, but it is possible that removing the infected fat can
finally eradicate the problem.

Cellulitis is possibly the worst side effect of lymphoedema, and
we need to better understand what causes such frequent bouts so
that we can improve both treatment and prevention. But what about
what causes the lymphoedema in the first place? There are a variety
of different reasons the lymph system can fail, which we'll look at
in the next chapter.

4

What Causes Lymphoedema?

Lymphoedema is essentially triggered by damage or disruption to lymph drainage, but there are many different causes of this damage, which fall into two categories: primary lymphoedema and secondary lymphoedema.

When the condition occurs without any warning, with no known interference to the lymph system from an outside source, it is called *primary* lymphoedema. In these cases, it is assumed that the lymph system has failed to form properly in the first place so that it therefore possesses a structural or functional weakness. This implies a genetic cause for the condition.

If there is an identifiable cause arising outside the lymph system interfering with lymph drainage, for example the removal of lymph glands in cancer treatment, this is called *secondary* lymphoedema.

GENES

Our genes play a part in many diseases, and lymphoedema is no exception. For patients whose lymphoedema has started without identifiable damage to lymph drainage it is likely there has been some pre-existing, presumed genetic, weakness of the lymph system, which effectively programmes it to fail.

This genetic trait might be inherited from parents, particularly if there is a history of the condition in the family. In such cases, lymphoedema can affect the child before he or she is even born. Swelling can sometimes be seen on the ultrasound scan during the pregnancy. However, more often than not the problem is only identified after birth.

Genetic testing can be used to determine whether a particular mutation is present or not. For example, in Milroy's Disease, which causes foot lymphoedema from birth and is usually inherited, a mutation in the gene known as *VEGFR3* can be detected in 70 per cent of cases. Finding such a mutation confirms the diagnosis without doubt. While identifying which gene is responsible does not provide any magical solution, it does give insights into the underlying biology and mechanisms that cause the lymphoedema, which could lead to the development of a cure.

It is naturally distressing for parents to find that their child has lymphoedema. However, understanding the condition and knowing what to expect in the future is very important if parents are to deal with it effectively. Genetic counselling is very helpful in these circumstances, and parents can be advised on the risk of having another child affected by lymphoedema and so plan their family accordingly.

Inheriting a mutation does not necessarily mean that lymphoedema will develop. Sometimes the mutation can remain 'silent' but still be passed on to future generations. Or it may not reveal itself immediately – symptoms might start showing at puberty, or sometimes even later:

Margaret was thirty-eight and had noticed swelling of her left ankle for twelve months. It ached a little and was uncomfortable by the end of the day, by which time her shoe felt noticeably tight.

Initially she assumed that she had somehow sprained her ankle, but after a month she went to her GP who immediately sent her off to the hospital to make sure she did not have a DVT (deep vein thrombosis). The scan was negative so she was referred to an orthopaedic surgeon. He arranged an X-ray and then a MRI scan in case there was an underlying fracture or soft tissue injury, but nothing was found other than fluid. She was discharged back to her GP who, in view of the fluid, gave a water tablet known as a diuretic. This made Margaret pass a lot of urine but did little to help the swelling. She was then referred to a vascular specialist who deals with the circulation. He organised a vein scan looking for varicose veins but again the results came back normal. He then suggested the swelling might be lymphoedema and recommended a stocking to wear.

In Margaret's case, there was no obvious outside cause for her lymphoedema, which means that it is likely she had a genetic weakness that led to the development of the condition later in life. This lack of an outside cause also contributed to the difficulties in diagnosing the cause of her swelling – difficulties which will be recognisable to many lymphoedema sufferers (see Chapter 6). When questioned by her therapist, Margaret did recall getting some swelling of her ankle after a flight to Australia some years previously but it had soon settled down. The swelling would also sometimes occur in extreme heat but it always recovered and she did not think anything of it. With hindsight, these were early signs of the lymph system struggling to work properly.

Not all genetic forms of lymphoedema are inherited; the genetic mutation might develop after the egg has formed. In these cases, the mutation generally only affects some cells in the body, a so-called mosaic genetic condition, and so the lymphoedema usually affects just one leg or one side of the body, whereas an inherited mutation will often produce symmetrical lymphoedema (i.e., both legs). Mosaic forms of lymphoedema are not usually passed on to offspring.

Genetic faults may also produce a lymph malformation or 'birthmark' abnormality of the lymph system. The vessels do not form properly, and lymph gets stuck inside them, unable to drain away, and so causes a swelling. This is a different swelling from lymphoedema as the lymph fluid remains within the malformed lymph vessels and not in the tissues, but sometimes the malformation interferes with nearby lymph drainage and so causes lymphoedema as well.

IMMOBILITY

It's possible that lymphoedema has become far more common in recent centuries. Modern humans spend far too much time sitting or standing still, and it makes us more prone to conditions such as varicose veins and swelling. Thousands of years ago, in the era of the hunter-gatherer, we would have spent most of our time either moving or lying down.

Gravity discourages both upward drainage of blood in our veins and lymph drainage up our legs. As soon as we stand up the veins in our legs fill, forcing fluid from the veins into the tissues of the legs. Under normal circumstances, movement then stimulates the lymph system to drain that fluid. However, if you spend a lot of time sitting in a chair, gravity continues to impede the regular flow of blood and lymph, engorging the veins in our legs. This causes an overflow of fluid into the legs, which will lead to swelling unless it is dealt with by the lymph system.

People who are infirm and unable to move properly often sit with their legs angled down for long periods. Without movement, lymph drainage is poor, and that combined with a high overflow of fluid results in worse and worse swelling over time.

We also don't move much when we sleep, so our lymph flow also drops then. However, while we are lying down, the fluid load on the lymph system in the legs and arms is also kept low, so the lymph system can cope and leg swelling will still improve overnight. So lying down is very important for giving our legs some respite from the constant effect of gravity.

OLD AGE

As we get older, the likelihood of developing lymphoedema grows. This may have something to do with an increasing lack of mobility, but it is also likely that, like most things in our body, the lymph system does not improve with age, just as the heart does not pump as effectively as we get older.

The symptoms of lymphoedema can appear quite gradually as we age; it is very common, for example, for older people to experience swollen ankles with increasing persistence. These symptoms may not cause much of a problem at first, and are often dismissed as relatively routine and harmless, but if they go untreated, as they often do, they can have an impact on mobility, lead to falls, prevent injuries from healing, cause fluid to leak from the skin, or lead to infection.

Claire is sixty-nine and in reasonable health. She does not drink or smoke but is somewhat overweight. At a routine check-up she was found to have slightly high blood pressure, for which she was prescribed some pills and advised to lose weight and exercise more. She found this difficult because she had arthritis in her left knee, which was affecting her mobility.

Sometime later she noticed her ankles beginning to swell but didn't pay much attention – partly because they did not hurt and partly because she was experiencing increasing pain in her knee. She found herself having to use a stick and was no longer able to manage parts of her weekly routine such as supermarket shopping. As a result, she spent more time sitting in a chair.

Claire's left ankle gradually became painful, red and increasingly swollen, and she began to notice similar symptoms in her right leg too. Her GP suspected that she had an infection and prescribed antibiotics, which had no effect. Claire was then given a different set of blood pressure tablets in case the original ones were causing the swelling. Her symptoms improved a little, but it was only when she became more mobile after a knee replacement and managed to lose some weight that the swelling properly began to subside. She nevertheless continues to have some swelling to this day.

It is so important to stay as active and mobile as possible as we get older, and to pay attention to changes in our bodies. Claire's swelling was only minor to begin with but eventually her lymph system became exhausted by the constant demands on it and she was left with permanent lymphoedema.

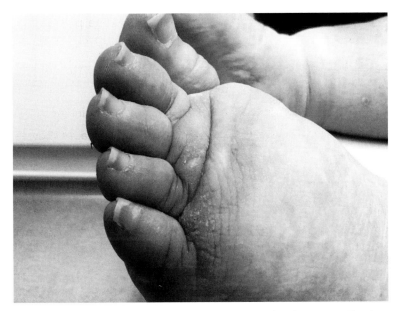

Poor mobility and long periods spent sitting can make lymphoedema worse. The skin soon becomes thicker with cracks and crevices that harbour germs, increasing the risk of infection.

OBESITY

People who are obese tend to move less and find movement increasingly difficult as they gain weight, which is one of the reasons obesity causes lymphoedema. The weight of a large stomach resting on the thighs when sitting also obstructs the flow of both blood in the veins and lymph to the lymph glands in the groin. Consequently pressure builds in the veins and lymph vessels, causing the legs to swell.

However, obesity also directly undermines lymph drainage for reasons not fully understood. In one clinical trial, for example, overweight patients were offered a variety of weight reduction diets to treat breast-cancer-related lymphoedema, which had caused one arm to swell up. All the patients who lost weight found that their swollen arm reduced in size over and above that of the other arm.

Rani Nagarajah, a dietician specialising in dietary treatments for lymphoedema, believes that the association between obesity and lymphoedema may have something to do with the nature of fat tissue itself:

> The problem with fat is that it has very few lymph vessels within it, so it is very poor at moving fluid onwards. The lean muscles do their best to exert pressure when you are exercising but moving fluid within fat is like trying to squeeze a tube of toothpaste when wearing oven gloves.
>
> The closer the lean muscles are to the lymph vessels the more efficient they can be, so keeping fat tissue to a minimum is always going to help, and losing weight will be beneficial for preventing and reducing all forms of lymphoedema – but only in those who are overweight.
>
> A significant gain in weight will also make existing lymphoedema worse. Obesity and lymphoedema can therefore become a vicious circle: obesity makes swelling worse, which impairs mobility, which burns fewer calories resulting in additional weight gain.

ACCIDENTAL TRAUMA OR SURGERY

Any accidental or surgical damage to lymph channels risks causing lymphoedema. Surgical removal of lymph glands is the most documented cause, such as happens with cancer treatment (see page 33), but lymphoedema can result after extensive surgery of any kind that damages or removes lymph vessels.

We know a lot about the recovery of blood vessels when they are damaged. For example, when you cut your finger, the blood soon clots and plugs the hole in the small blood vessels, known as capillaries, to stop the bleeding. These blood capillaries then sprout tiny new capillaries to replace the damaged ones.

Where there are blood capillaries, there are also lymph vessels. If you cut your finger, these tiny lymph vessels will also be damaged, and they repair themselves in much the same way as blood capillaries.

It is inevitable, therefore, that surgery involves severing lymph vessels, and on a much larger scale than a cut to your finger. If the surgical cut is small then the surviving lymph vessels nearby take on the responsibility of maintaining lymph drainage. However if the surgical cut is large, there may be extensive damage to the vessels and new ones must be grown. The problem is that newly formed lymph vessels struggle to grow through scar tissue, therefore the bigger the surgical cut or traumatic injury the more likely local lymph drainage will be affected.

If the surgery involves the removal of one or more lymph glands, the effects can be more serious. This is because lymph glands are positioned at points where multiple lymph vessels converge, and so their removal can have wider ramifications. This is why cancer treatment commonly causes lymphoedema (see below).

CANCER TREATMENT

Not many people know what lymphoedema is, but those who do often believe that cancer is its main cause. However, it is the treatment of cancer rather than the disease itself that causes the problem.

As we have seen, lymph glands act as filtering stations for every-thing that leaves the body's tissues via the lymph system (see page 6). This includes cancer cells, which, if gathered in sufficient numbers, will reproduce rapidly and then spread. Cancer therefore tends to spread through the body via the lymph system – and it is the spread of cancer that is fatal. If you have cancer in your left breast, for example, it is most likely to spread to the lymph glands in your left armpit.

Unfortunately, the treatments designed to stop this process can damage the lymph system. Radiotherapy, some types of chemotherapies and the surgical removal of even just one lymph gland can all contribute to lymphoedema, as Professor Kefah Mokbel, a consultant breast surgeon, explains:

Current breast cancer treatment requires the surgical removal of lymph glands from the armpit in order to find out if the cancer has spread to them or not. This can lead to lymphoedema in the arm, and the more lymph glands removed, the greater the risk.

Years ago it was customary to remove most, if not all, of the lymph glands in the armpit as a curative treatment for breast cancer. Nowadays, that is reserved for women whose cancer has clearly spread to the glands there (which can be determined through clinical examination or ultrasound imaging of the glands). Most women will now go through a selective and accurate sampling of the regional lymph glands, called the sentinel lymph node biopsy.

The sentinel lymph node is the first lymph gland in the armpit to which cancer spreads. If the sentinel gland is free of cancer then the other glands in the armpit down the line are likely to be as well, in which case there is no need to remove them. If significant numbers of cancer cells are found in the sentinel gland then standard practice is to remove all, or most, of the remaining lymph glands from the armpit or treat them with radiotherapy. The scientific evidence clearly demonstrates that the more extensive the surgery in the armpit, the higher the risk of lymphoedema. However, radiotherapy is not without risk either.

Although the armpit is the main route for spread of breast cancer cells, the lymph glands above the collar-bone can often be involved as well. These glands are not surgically sampled or removed but are usually treated with radiotherapy. Many of us remember the effects of super doses of radiotherapy that were used in the 1980s in an attempt to cure breast cancer. Such was the severity of the long-term side effects, including arm lymphoedema, that the issue was raised in Parliament. The patient advocacy group Radiation Action Group Exposure (RAGE) campaigned about it vigorously, which led to the problem being recognised and improvements in patient care.

However, until cancer treatment avoids lymph gland removal or radiotherapy, the risk of developing lymphoedema will always remain.

There was a time when chemotherapy was considered irrelevant for lymphoedema risk but not any more. Chemotherapy is used most often to reduce the chances of cancer recurring after surgery and radiotherapy. It can sometimes be used before surgery or radiotherapy to increase the chances of cure; or it can be used to treat cancer known to have spread to parts of the body outside the reach of surgery or radiotherapy. It appears likely that taxanes, a widely used chemotherapy agent, increase the lymph load by making blood vessels in the arm release more fluid. This can overwhelm a lymph system already weakened by lymph gland removal and so cause lymphoedema.

Lymphoedema in the arm is the most common form following breast cancer treatment, however, with the advent of minimalist surgery, the problem of breast lymphoedema has emerged, although it has received much less attention. With a mastectomy, when the whole breast is removed, breast oedema is clearly not a problem. However, these days, where possible, standard treatment is a 'lumpectomy' or wide local excision, to conserve the breast for aesthetic reasons. This increases the chance of breast cancer returning, though, so radiotherapy is used on the breast as well.

Radiotherapy has an effect like sunburn and causes inflammation of the breast and overlying skin. Lymph flow through the skin is reduced, and that, combined with the removal of lymph glands in the area, causes fluid to build up in the breast. Sometimes the lymph vessels do not fully recover after the 'sunburn' effect of the radiotherapy has subsided, resulting in lymphoedema. Breast lymphoedema is uncomfortable at best, and painful at worst. It also makes the breast susceptible to cellulitis, and it leads to a lop-sided cosmetic effect, which may be difficult to hide under clothing if the swelling is severe. The good news is that if infection can be prevented and treatment pursued, the breast lymphoedema can eventually resolve.

Lymphoedema is, of course, not only caused by treatment for breast cancer. All types of cancer, from gynaecological to skin cancer, are treated in similar ways and so can lead to the development of the condition in the treated area, whether in the arm or leg, or less commonly in the genitals or face and neck (see page 159).

A man suffering from filariasis, which is also known as elephantiasis because the swollen leg resembles that of an elephant.

INFECTION

We've already seen that infection is a major problem for sufferers of lymphoedema (see Chapter 3), but an infection can also be the cause. A bacterial infection of the lymph vessels or skin can harm vulnerable lymph vessels and disrupt lymph flow, thereby leading to the condition. A vicious circle can therefore become established whereby an infection causes lymphoedema, which leads to further attacks of infection such as cellulitis, which in turn make the lymphoedema worse and so on.

FILARIASIS

Filariasis is a parasitic disease carried by blood-feeding black flies and mosquitoes. If you are bitten by an infected insect, worm larvae can be deposited on your skin and make their way into your body and on into your lymph system. The disease, which is also called elephantiasis, affects people living in tropical and sub-tropical climates, and although it is not a life-threatening infection it can cause lasting damage to the lymph system resulting in swelling of the leg or genitalia.

Filariasis, although common, is classed as a neglected tropical disease, as is podoconiosis, another form of lymphoedema found in the tropics. Both are discussed in more detail in Chapter 13.

DEEP VEIN THROMBOSIS

A deep vein thrombosis (DVT) is a blood clot that develops within a deep vein, usually in the leg. The resulting blockage in blood flow causes a sudden rise of pressure in the affected veins so forcing extra fluid out from the blood stream and into the tissues of the leg. Unless the lymph system can cope with this extra fluid then it will lead to acute swelling. Usually this swelling subsides once the clot has been cleared using blood thinners, but it can sometimes persist. When this occurs, it is almost certainly, in part, due to additional damage to the lymph drainage from the thrombosis. Persistent swelling of a leg after a DVT is called 'post-thrombotic syndrome' but is, in essence, lymphoedema.

VARICOSE VEINS

Varicose veins are stretched tortuous veins that are engorged with blood because they are not emptying properly. Pressure builds within the varicose veins when you are sitting or standing, forcing fluid into the tissues – a good deal more fluid than would be expected from normal veins. Unless the lymph drainage is robust and capable of dealing with this extra fluid, oedema will occur. Because varicose veins usually occur in the legs, the associated swelling usually occurs at its worst in the foot and ankle, where the pressure in the veins is at its highest.

The main way to give respite to the affected veins is elevation, which collapses the veins and lowers the pressure within them. You can see this for yourself by sitting down in bare feet and observing the veins around the ankles and tops of feet bulge. If you then lie down and raise your foot above heart level, the veins collapse, meaning that much less fluid is released from the veins into the tissues. This allows the lymph system time to catch up with its fluid drainage responsibilities.

Surgery for varicose veins will often reduce the swelling but if it does not then the cause is probably lymphoedema. Furthermore, as lymph vessels are positioned anatomically very close to surface veins in the leg, any surgical treatment of varicose veins can damage the lymph vessels as well:

Rita is fifty-three but first noticed varicose veins in her left leg when she was at university. At that time she had the standard treatment, which was to strip out the unwanted varicose veins, but like her mother, who also had treatment for varicose veins, Rita found that the unsightly veins slowly returned. At the age of forty she sought further treatment and had laser destruction of the veins, but again they returned. This time, however, the problem affected multiple small surface veins, accompanied by some brown staining in the skin around the ankle and some oedema. Despite two more attempts to treat the veins the oedema only got worse.

Rita's story – and her mother's experience – also points to a genetic factor in varicose veins. There is known to be a significant cross-over between the genes governing the development of lymph vessels and those that affect veins, so if your veins are inherently weak – and susceptible to becoming varicose – there might also be a similar weakness in your lymph vessels, which could in turn make you more susceptible to lymphoedema.

So we can see that there are many different causes of lymphoedema, some of which are more easily avoidable than others, and some of which are much more common than others. We still don't know all the risk factors involved in developing the condition in each instance, but we can look at the available statistics to assess how common lymphoedema really is, and which causes present the biggest risks.

5

How Common Is Lymphoedema?

According to recent estimates, lymphoedema is as common as Alzheimer's disease, four times as common as HIV and rheumatoid arthritis, and twelve times as common as multiple sclerosis. However, determining the exact numbers of people affected by lymphoedema is not easy.

One problem is that lymphoedema is difficult to diagnose – not all people with oedema are suffering from lymphoedema and it can be hard to pinpoint the difference. Someone who suffers from occasional swelling probably doesn't have the condition, but if it becomes permanent and uncomfortable then a failing lymph system should certainly be considered. In this respect, diagnosing lymphoedema is a little bit like diagnosing cognitive impairment: we can all suffer memory lapses, particularly as we get older, but that doesn't mean we are necessarily suffering from dementia unless it becomes a continuous problem.

Another problem is the relative lack of research on lymphoedema, which means that studies and statistics are not as readily available or complete as they are for other diseases. Most of the information we do have relates to breast cancer, as that is the area in which most of the studies have been done, but to understand the full burden of lymphoedema in societies we have to look beyond this narrow association.

Professor Christine Moffatt is one of the few people in the world to have studied this. In 2001 she performed a survey in South West

Lymphoedema is more common in older people, but it can affect the young as well. Tanya puts on a brave and cheerful face despite the problems the lymphoedema in her left leg causes her.

London in the UK investigating chronic oedema (which is essentially the same thing as lymphoedema). She found that for every 1,000 people in the general population, there were 1.33 cases, but this figure rose to 5.4 in people over sixty-five. In 2012 a similar study was carried out further north in the UK in the town of Derby, which found that there were 4.0 cases for every 1,000 people in the general population. At first sight, this suggests that lymphoedema is more common in Derby than in London. This might well be true for reasons that are not yet known, but a more likely explanation is that methods for identifying patients were more robust in the second study. The Derby figure is probably therefore more accurate.

The study in Derby also confirmed that lymphoedema is more common among the elderly; it found approximately 10 in every 1,000 people aged between sixty-five and seventy-four were affected with lymphoedema, and in those over eighty-five this figure rose to nearly 30.

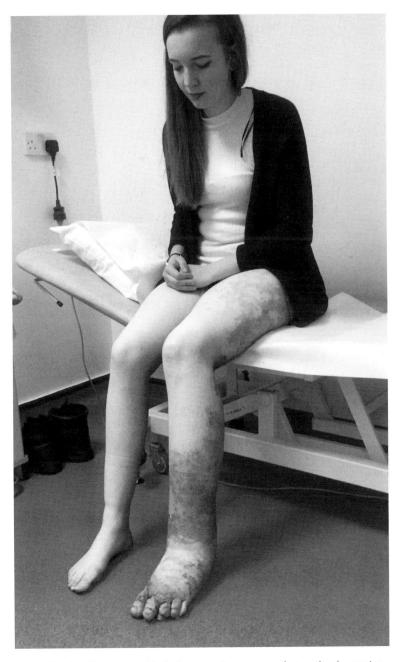

Primary lymphoedema, caused by faulty genes, is uncommon but can be devastating for young people because of the physical and psychological disabilities that result.

As expected, due to its prevalence among breast cancer survivors, lymphoedema also proved to be twice as common in women as men. One in nine women has a lifetime risk of breast cancer, and one in five women treated for breast cancer has a lifetime risk of lymphoedema. So one does not have to be a mathematician to see that breast-cancer-related lymphoedema is relatively common. Lymphoedema in the lower limb from treatment of gynaecological or male urogenital cancers is just as common but has been studied less than breast cancer.

Cancer treatment is generally thought of as the main cause of lymphoedema, but Professor Moffat's studies have indicated that this is true for less than one in four cases. Obesity (and/or reduced mobility) was identified as the sole cause in at least 26 per cent of cases, and it was also found to be a contributing factor in other cases. Interestingly, primary lymphoedema (where the failure in the lymph system appears to be built-in from birth) was found in 12 per cent of all cases, making it much more common than generally realised.

In another study, all in-patients at a main city hospital and community hospital were examined during a forty-eight-hour period. Of 453 people assessed, 129 (28.5 per cent) were found to have lymphoedema, a staggering statistic. Of course most were not admitted directly as a result of their condition, but this merely reveals the complex health issues that sufferers of lymphoedema tend to face.

Worldwide, one of the most common causes of lymphoedema is filariasis (see pages 37 and 175). It occurs in tropical climates only, but the World Health Organisation estimates that 120 million people are infected with the disease and of those, 40 million have lymphoedema or another related problem such as hydrocele (lymph fluid collecting in the sac around the testicles).

THE RISK FACTORS

It is difficult to predict who may develop lymphoedema; obesity may be a common cause, but what is the actual likelihood of developing lymphoedema if a person is obese? At the moment we don't know, and again, most of the existing research has been conducted in relation to breast cancer. But the risk is certainly known to be high if there is a family history. Consultant breast surgeon Professor Kefah Mokbel explains why some people are more at risk than others after cancer treatment:

> It is unclear why some people develop lymphoedema after cancer treatment and not others. It can sometimes seem very random. For example, the majority of women who have all the lymph glands removed from their armpit do not develop it, yet 5 per cent of women who have only one lymph gland removed do. Some people get it immediately after their treatment, and others not for many months or years.
>
> However, there are definitely some factors that increase the likelihood of developing lymphoedema. First, the extent of the surgery and, in particular, having more lymph glands removed; second, radiotherapy, and especially treatment of the armpit; third, an infection immediately after surgery can add further damage to already vulnerable lymph drainage routes; fourth, being overweight – the greater the weight the greater the risk of lymphoedema (see page 31). Unfortunately sometimes it is the cancer treatment that leads to weight gain, often caused by the steroids that are commonly given with chemotherapy in order to reduce side effects, and it can be difficult to lose this weight, even long after the course of steroids is over. Weight gain is also

one of the side effects of hormonal therapy, which is often given long term (five to ten years) to discourage return of the breast cancer.

Despite these factors, who gets lymphoedema after breast cancer treatment is still very unpredictable. It is thought that abnormal physiology is far more complicated than realised, as it doesn't develop just because of obstructed lymph drainage in the armpit.

Recent studies have shown women who went on to develop lymphoedema actually had higher levels of lymph drainage in their arms before surgery. The lymph vessels appear to be working harder and pumping at higher pressures in those predisposed to lymphoedema. The problem appears to be as much about the extra fluid load on a lymph system made vulnerable by surgery as it is about a blocked lymph system.

Everything points to an existing predisposition to lymphoedema, which may be genetic. Identifying these at-risk women before they embark on cancer treatment could be the way forward to prevent lymphoedema.

Understanding exactly why and how lymphoedema develops, and who is at risk, is essential if we are to find a cure, or better still prevent it. The lack of information can be frustrating. Without clear statistics on how common the different causes are, it can be hard to establish the risks involved with any certainty. If we're to help patients, we need more research, and for that to happen, we have to raise awareness of lymphoedema – especially among doctors and other healthcare professionals.

6

Awareness and Diagnosis

Lymphoedema is one of the few conditions where the informed patient can often know more about it than their doctor. This is because the importance of the lymph system has not been fully appreciated until recently and little attention is given to it in medical school and healthcare teaching.

RAISING AWARENESS

William Repicci is President and CEO of the Lymphatic Education & Research Network (LE&RN), a nonprofit organisation based in New York. As he explains, LE&RN's mission is to fight lymphatic diseases and lymphoedema through education, research and advocacy:

> When I was asked to join the lymphatic field, I posed an initial query: why was lymphoedema, of which I knew little, deserving of my attention? My search for an answer proved transformational.
>
> I was most surprised to learn that as many as 150 million people worldwide were estimated to have lymphoedema. I became curious as to why I was well-versed in diseases such as multiple sclerosis, Parkinson's, amyotrophic lateral sclerosis, muscular dystrophy and AIDS, and yet was ignorant about a disease which affects more people in the United

'Despite all the consideration that we give to cancer, lymphoedema, which often results from cancer treatment, receives little attention. Our experience suggests that when an affliction receives publicity and public engagement, unforeseen progress can be made. '

Michael Portillo

States than all these diseases combined. Lymphoedema had my attention.

LE&RN is dedicated to advancing the world's scientific understanding of lymphatic diseases. However, research costs money and what limited funding there is goes to those who clamour the loudest. When it came to lymphoedema, there was a curious silence. If I wanted to succeed, I first needed to unravel the puzzle of how millions of people across the globe could be muted on an issue where their health and well-being were concerned.

The lymph system was discovered in the seventeenth century, but the difficulties in viewing it, which limited our understanding of how it works and what it does, kept it largely off the radar. In recent times, interest in the lymph system has been buoyed by a handful of advocates and researchers due to improved techniques of investigation; however, there is little funding available to keep researchers invested in the field. Government funders tend to respond to the priorities of the populace, so this begs the question: why hasn't the patient population demanded attention?

Generally, if we have an ailment, we see our doctor and in time we are told its name. We then begin our search for additional information, resources and a support network. And, in need of understanding and compassion, we confide in family and friends. Unfortunately, all too often this is not the way things unfold for the lymphoedema patient. One of the biggest complaints they have is that they were either undiagnosed or misdiagnosed for years after first visiting a medical practitioner.

The conundrum here is that we need informed medical practitioners. However, without medical treatments to teach their students, universities and board exams pay too little attention to this disease. With lymphoedema largely overlooked by medical schools, doctors enter the field with scant knowledge of this lymphatic disease, its incidence and its symptoms. So, rather than patients being told that they have lymphoedema, they are often informed that they suffer from 'drainage issues' or 'poor circulation' or that they simply need to lose weight.

Using the correct language is important; it allows people to seek out information and locate resources. Knowing the name of your disease connects you with others who suffer similarly. There is power in numbers when trying to create change. With patients disconnected from one another, denied a diagnosis with a name, the history of lymphoedema proves that even a disease of epidemic proportions can be kept invisible. Furthermore, instead of looking for support for their unnamed ailment, patients tend to hide the disease, perhaps worried that no one cares about a disease without a name. The result is that family and friends are at a loss either to understand or provide necessary comfort. And it is common for lymphoedema patients to admit that they have never met another person who has lymphoedema, and, in many cases, that they believe they are the only person suffering from this disease.

So, for starters, lymphoedema and lymphatic diseases are under-researched, which leads to few treatments. As a result, medical schools feel there is little to teach, doctors are left uninformed, patients are isolated with an undiagnosed disease, researchers are unaware of the need, and research funders are focused elsewhere.

To further complicate the issue, there are many rare lymphatic diseases with names that leave both the patient and public unaware of their lymphatic connection. The National Institutes of Health (NIH) in the USA estimates that between 1 in 6000 to 1 in 300 are born with one of these primary lymphatic diseases (lymphoedema or some sort of lymph disorder). The broad discrepancy in these estimates is telling in itself, revealing that even our scientific watchdogs are unsure of the precise incidence.

Proteus syndrome, for example, is a rare disease affecting fewer than 150 people worldwide. It was brought to popular attention by the play, and later the film, *The Elephant Man*, which tells the story of Joseph Merrick. Yet, despite the widespread success this story had on stage and screen, people would probably be surprised to hear that Mr Merrick suffered from a lymphatic disease. Other primary lymphatic diseases without the benefit of literary celebrities go by names unrecognised by most. Again, it is hard to build a collective movement when advocates for rare diseases either don't recognise or acknowledge their common lymphatic link. Focusing on one syndrome does provide much-needed attention for that syndrome. However, it can leave researchers as the ones making the case for the importance of broad-based lymphatic research, whereas patient advocates might be far more effective.

The last piece of the puzzle which helps to keep lymphoedema awareness out of the mainstream is easy to understand and yet perhaps the most formidable to overcome. Globally, the majority of people with lymphoedema in western society are perceived to be cancer survivors, and in the developing world they are mainly those who have contracted filariasis. The former are from industrialised nations with advanced healthcare. The latter are almost exclusively from tropical countries where healthcare is lacking. In both cases, societal and psychosocial dynamics play roles in keeping lymphoedema under the radar.

In industrial countries, little is heard of the millions with filarial lymphoedema. In tropical areas plagued by filariasis, people report a stigma associated with the disease. Living in fear of being socially ostracised as a lymphoedema patient with filariasis, even patients with non-filarial lymphoedema remain silent and refrain from seeking treatment.

In countries with advanced healthcare, secondary lymphoedema is on the rise as successful cancer treatment leads to a higher survival rate. Thus, you might expect that lymphoedema would routinely become part of the conversation when medical professionals discuss cancer with patients. Patients, however, report that this has not been the case. In great numbers, they state that they were never informed about the possible side-effects of lymphoedema prior to cancer treatment. Since a significant number of those cancer survivors were likely to get lymphoedema, what did doctors tell their patients once symptoms occurred?

Within a few days of assuming my position with LE&RN, I got my answer from two women who had developed lymphoedema as a result of cancer treatment. I asked them what it was like to have the disease. 'There are worse things in the world,' they said. When I responded that I was perhaps then wasting my time in this field, they paused, and asked: 'Do you really want to know what lymphoedema is like?'

What followed was a long, heart-wrenching story in which they listed the myriad ways lymphoedema impacted their lives on a daily basis – both physically and psychosocially. They began by asking me to imagine what it would feel like to be carrying ten pounds of weight in one extremity, but not in the corresponding limb. Stories were shared of loss of exercise, the abandoning of once-loved activities, their fear that air travel and high altitudes would exacerbate swelling, their vigilance in dealing with regular bouts of cellulitis that resulted in visits to hospital emergency rooms, and their loss of physical intimacy with a loved one. They shared stories of being stopped on the street by strangers who chastised them for their weight, or of being turned away by restaurant maître d's who feared they would upset other patrons. Forsaking all reserve, they then delivered their definitive declaration. 'Lymphoedema is worse than cancer. They cured my cancer. Lymphoedema is forever.'

This interaction began to answer my question as to why a disease that affects so many had not become a worldwide priority. After hearing all of the ways these women's lives had been affected by the disease, I asked them why they were so resistant to sharing the full truth of their story? One woman answered: 'My doctor told me he cured my cancer, that lymphoedema wouldn't kill me, and that I should just be grateful and not complain.'

Of course it is true that lymphoedema is not usually a fatal disease in itself, but it often leads to complications that can prove fatal or which can significantly shorten life. However, I asked myself, why is there even a need to make this case? There are hosts of diseases that have received our collective attention that do not lead to reduced lifespan. Dying before one's time is tragic. But it is equally tragic to live a tortured life without a day's respite from suffering.

If we address each of the identified obstacles, we can begin to make the fight against lymphoedema and lymphatic diseases a global priority. But winning this battle means that all those who suffer from these diseases, and those who love them, must jump to the front lines of this fight. This battle is best won if those with primary and secondary lymphoedema, filarial lymphoedema and lymphatic diseases join in one collective movement. Change occurs when an empowered critical mass of people demand it. This doesn't occur if patients are kept from bonding with one another because their disease is going undiagnosed or isn't given a name. This doesn't occur if the medical practitioners convince patients that their suffering isn't worthy of society's attention. Patients need to come forward and decry the perverse notion that they should stay invisible or in the shadow of their disease.

For patients to rise up, they first need to feel hope. The utter lack of hope among people with lymphoedema was made clear by a phone call I received in response to LE&RN's research agenda. 'Bill, you are wasting your time,' the caller told me. 'They will never find a cure for lymphoedema.' My heart sank at hearing these words, and it sank still further when she went on to say that her one dream in life was to feel normal for just one day before she died.

We cannot create an army out of people who have no anticipation of victory. Research has not given them a cure, and NGOs have failed to inspire their confidence in a future with new treatments. When I spoke to the woman who suggested we abandon our research efforts, I asked her to think back to the 1980s, when a new disease had just emerged. Researchers knew nothing about it and it had no name. But now, thanks to those who fought for AIDS research to become a worldwide priority, it has become a treatable disease. If we persevere, we must believe the same will occur in the fight against the current lymphoedemic. It was thanks to the stories and insights shared with me by so many, that my transformation from neophyte to impassioned advocate became complete.

Every movement needs leaders to galvanise its members. In the case of lymphoedema, Academy Award-winner, LE&RN spokesperson, and lymphoedema patient Kathy

Bates has emerged as a lightning rod for the lymphoedema community (see page 124). In addition, NGOs worldwide spearhead advocacy efforts, such as LE&RN establishing the first World Lymphoedema Day on 6 March 2016. As dozens of countries join in a collective movement, the sense of isolation abates. Our strength in numbers energises us. Our unwavering conviction is that lymphoedema and lymphatic diseases are international priorities. We must believe that treatments and cures will occur in strong measure because we will not accept anything less than this. The world cannot ignore the voice of 150 million people who refuse to be silenced. We need to help each one of those individuals find her and his unique voice and lend that voice to this fight.

CHALLENGES FOR GENERAL PRACTITIONERS

This lack of awareness obviously causes problems for the patient, but it of course presents a challenge to GPs as well – a challenge made all the harder by the conditions in which they have to work.

GPs are expected to know everything for all patients – an impossible task. They have little time to see patients; therefore they need to diagnose a problem and treat it as quickly as possible. In practice, this means ruling out the most likely/obvious things first, but given the lack of training that all medical students receive on the lymph system, a diagnosis of lymphoedema is rarely a consideration for GPs. When they see a swollen ankle, they are more likely to consider an injury or a thrombosis (DVT) as an explanation. Deep vein thrombosis is admittedly an important diagnosis, so it is correct to refer a patient to hospital for a Doppler examination but not if the patient has had swelling for months. Even when a thrombosis is excluded, lymphoedema is still not usually considered. Fluid retention often causes swelling, so as a next step a doctor will usually prescribe diuretics or 'water tablets', which may well help other forms of oedema, but not lymphoedema.

Dr Jonathan Moore, a GP in the Cotswolds, explains the frustrations a doctor faces when it comes to recognising lymphoedema and knowing what steps to take next:

When seeing an elderly patient 'with swollen legs', a GP is faced with certain difficulties, as there can be many reasons for the swelling. The most important thing to do first is to rule out a serious cause like a blood clot. The next step is to exclude an infection – often a patient's legs are red, indicating that is a possibility, so the dutiful GP will give a week's course of antibiotics to address it and hope it will get better.

If nothing has improved then the question is, what to do next? We are taught that there are three options; elevation, compression and, failing that, 'water tablets'. Asking the patient to elevate their legs may be very effective in the short term, but the swelling will almost always return so this is rarely a practical long-term solution.

The GP may then offer 'compression stockings'. In the hands of an expert these can be very useful; but for anyone else, the successful application and fitting can be very hit and miss. A practice nurse may have had training, but often patients get them fitted at a pharmacy, and I am uncertain how much training an average pharmacist has. A crudely applied pressure stocking is often very uncomfortable and patients who don't fully understand the benefits are not keen to use it as a long-term treatment. The stockings can

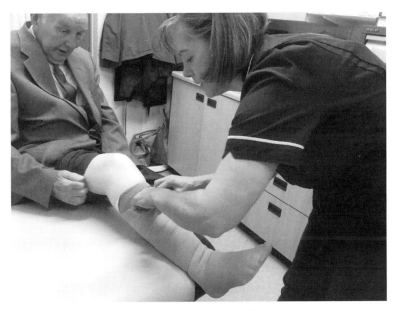

Swollen legs in the elderly are a common problem for GPs. Bandages or support stockings are the correct treatment but they are often difficult to manage unless trained staff are available.

also be difficult to get on and off, and it's certainly not an easy undertaking if you are old and racked with arthritis.

If this treatment has failed the patient is offered 'water tablets'. For certain conditions like heart failure this is appropriate and works well. However for chronic swelling and lymphoedema this is very unlikely to work because the swelling is not just due to fluid, and so water tablets do not improve lymph drainage.

At this point both patient and GP can become despondent. The great difficulty is that there is not an easy way to refer a patient to an expert, and this is what is most needed at this stage. The causes of lymphoedema are complex and each patient needs careful assessment and treatment for the specific cause in their case.

As Dr Moore says, even when a diagnosis of lymphoedema has been made, there is a lack of specialists to whom patients can be referred. Sometimes a GP might recommend an ultrasound examination of the abdomen to ensure that there is no cancer obstructing lymph drainage. If that comes back negative then the patient might be referred to a vascular surgeon who deals with the blood circulation, but there is usually no surgery to offer for the lymph system. It can be a frustrating experience for all concerned, as Dr Moore goes on to make clear:

> Although lymphoedema is not curable, it is very treatable. Identifying the sometimes multiple underlying causes can be time consuming and frustrating, requiring patience from both the doctor and the sufferer, but by taking the time to do so, we can give the best chance of providing the best treatment. With an expert, multidisciplinary approach, with different health care professionals offering their various skills, over time it should be possible to make real progress.
>
> Sadly, nationally there does not exist a service that can properly address the needs of each patient. For a while the only specialist lymphoedema nurse in North Oxfordshire was based at the local hospice, and that was only as part of terminal care. A GP may refer to the hospital but it is unlikely that the patient will receive excellent care by a suitable specialist.
>
> With limited time, poor training and understanding of the condition it can be all too easy to apply poor, crude and over simplistic treatments to our patients. Unfortunately, while NHS resources remain so stretched it is unlikely extra

money will be spent on an expensive service for a condition which is ultimately not life threatening.

However, the reality remains that lymphoedema is a chronic long-term condition, which can be very disabling for its sufferers, who traditionally have been left to bear their affliction in silence. They shouldn't have to do so any longer.

DELAYS FOR THE PATIENT

All this might be frustrating for the doctor, but of course it is much worse for the patient, unable to obtain a diagnosis for their condition. Take Alan's story:

Alan is fifty-three years old; fourteen years ago he was on holiday in Turkey when he suffered a severe infection, known as cellulitis, in his right leg. He was admitted to hospital and treated with intravenous antibiotics and recovered, although the following year he suffered a similar infection.

No further problems arose until a year ago, when his right leg and ankle began to swell for no obvious reason. He was sent to hospital urgently, in case of a DVT (deep vein thrombosis) but tests proved negative. He was then sent to see an orthopaedic surgeon who arranged a MRI of the ankle. This revealed only fluid in the tissues (oedema) so he was reassured. He didn't feel unwell and wasn't in any pain but he was frustrated that nobody could tell him why his limb was swollen.

However, he suddenly became very sick with fever, vomiting and headaches, which are all symptoms of septicaemia. He was rushed off to hospital by ambulance. By this point, his right leg had become very painful, bright red and warm to the touch, indicating an infection. The emergency doctors treated him with intravenous antibiotics and the infection settled, but only slowly; it took three weeks of antibiotics in total. And even then, his leg and ankle were still swollen, and were worse than before the most recent infection.

It was only following this most recent infection that Alan was diagnosed with lymphoedema, but the signs were there from much earlier in his story. When he suffered the second attack of cellulitis in the same part of his right leg, for example, it should have alerted healthcare professionals to a possible problem with lymph drainage. Later, when the MRI scan revealed nothing but fluid in his swollen leg, this too should have brought lymphoedema into play as a possible diagnosis, but the truth is that doctors do not often consider lymph problems as an explanation for fluid. Usually what happens is that the patient is reassured and told that the fluid is harmless and will probably disappear on its own. And that, of course, is simply not true if it is caused by lymphoedema. This is exactly what happened to Alan, and nothing more was done until another debilitating infection occurred.

SCREENING AND EARLY DIAGNOSIS

Although there is no cure for lymphoedema, early diagnosis and treatment can significantly lessen its effects. In some cases, if caught early enough, the condition can even be prevented from developing fully – after breast cancer, for example, when the risk factors and early signs are more recognisable. One problem, however, is that cancer patients themselves aren't always made aware of the risks. Not only can the development of lymphoedema come as a nasty shock for those who think they are on the road to recovery after treatment, but it also means that they don't know the signs to look out for, which makes them slower to seek the necessary treatment.

Carmel Phelan, a lymphoedema therapist, often sees how distressing it is for patients to develop lymphoedema after cancer treatment:

It is always surprising to find that some patients have not heard of lymphoedema. Others are aware of it, but never realised they were at risk. Many express their anger at not being taken seriously by their cancer specialists, whether it is their surgeon, oncologist or breast care nurse. Patients sometimes complain several times of symptoms such as swelling, pain, aching, tightness or other symptoms that would indicate the possible onset of lymphoedema but nothing is done. In some cases, where lymphoedema has already developed, patients are told that it is 'normal' after surgery or cancer treatment, and that the swelling 'will go away in time'.

Of course the majority of patients treated for breast cancer do not develop lymphoedema, even those patients who have had all their lymph glands removed from their armpit. However, the removal of just one lymph gland does convey a lifetime risk of lymphoedema. People need to be made aware of the risk as early as possible, even before any lymph glands are removed, so they can seek advice from a lymphoedema practitioner or specialist and know what early signs to look out for. It is important to note at this point that early signs do not always involve swelling. Symptoms such as increased aching can also indicate lymphoedema. There are also some preventative measures that can be put in place – a light compression sleeve, for example, can be provided as a precaution when carrying out heavy or repetitive duties, performing intense arm exercise or travelling by air. In theory this should help with prevention, although the evidence supporting this practice is weak.

If the patient is aware of the risks, and swelling can be treated quickly, it can prevent the development of lymphoedema:

Catherine had her breast lump removed and within the same operation a lymph gland from the armpit was sampled. Thankfully, no cancer was found in the gland so no more lymph glands needed to be taken. Within a matter of days, before she was due to start chemo, her hand started to swell and her rings became tight. She knew of the risk of lymphoedema but had been told that it was highly unlikely. Fortunately a lymphoedema therapist saw her quickly and the swelling responded well to a compression glove, massage and an exercise programme. By the time she had completed her chemo and radiotherapy the swelling had all but disappeared.

As we've seen, it's not always easy to identify lymphoedema. Even after cancer treatment, the condition may not be considered if the swelling occurs after some time has passed. When it is diagnosed, it is very important to confirm it with proper tests – a misdiagnosis

'The extraordinary advances in medical science prove to us every day that conditions once thought of as impossible to treat have come well within the range of the wonderfully possible. To me that suggests that we should redouble our efforts to support projects raising awareness of conditions like lymphoedema.'

Sir Trevor McDonald

when the condition isn't present can be just as detrimental and disruptive to a person's lifestyle:

Rachel, a retired lady in her sixties and a keen amateur violin player, developed swelling, heaviness and aching in her arm after treatment for breast cancer. She was assessed by a lymphoedema practitioner who diagnosed the condition. She was told that this was a chronic, progressive, incurable disease, and she was given a compression garment to wear all day every day for the rest of her life. She was also warned against overusing her arm, so stopped playing in concerts.

Later Rachel had Indocyanine Green (ICG) lymphography (see below) to define the condition of her lymph vessels. This revealed normal-looking lymph vessels in both of her arms and the lymph appeared to be moving normally up the arm as well. In short, there was no evidence of lymphoedema and she was advised to stop wearing the compression sleeve, and go back to her normal activities.

Twelve months later, Rachel is back to playing four-hour concerts without any problem. The swelling hasn't returned and her ICG lymphography screening remains normal. Rachel has been empowered by an accurate diagnosis to take back control of her life.

ICG lymphography is one of only a handful of tests that can look at the lymph system with any degree of accuracy, which means that confirming a diagnosis of lymphoedema is not always straightforward. Blood tests and X-rays may be helpful to diagnose other conditions but they show up nothing in early stages of lymphoedema, while ultrasound examination, CT or MRI scans can show fluid but do not tell you why it is there.

The main test used is called lymphoscintigraphy – a name which many healthcare workers struggle to pronounce or remember! The procedure involves injecting a material tagged with a tiny amount of radioactivity (much, much less than is used in a CT scan) just under the skin in the hand or foot. A camera that detects the radioactivity can then view the material entering the lymph system and travelling up the lymph vessels to the lymph glands. Here the amount of material that accumulates can be measured and so indicate how good, or bad, the lymph drainage is in the whole limb. It can't, however, show the lymph vessels with much clarity. Lymphoscintigraphy is not available to GPs, only to hospital specialists, and even then it is not widely used, but techniques like this are key to making a correct diagnosis.

Professor Dominic Furniss and Alex Ramsden of the Oxford Lymphoedema Practice discuss other ways used to catch the condition as early as possible:

The first step in early diagnosis is defining who is at high risk of developing lymphoedema. Patients who have had their lymph glands removed or who have had radiotherapy or chemotherapy as part of cancer treatment are at high risk of developing secondary lymphoedema (see page 33).

For these high-risk patients, there are several methods of screening for lymphoedema. Most commonly, lymphoedema practitioners will use a combination of patient symptoms and limb volume measurements to make a diagnosis. This is fraught with difficulty, however, as distinguishing between post-operative swelling and lymphoedema can be problematic (as happened in Rachel's story). Also, no one has defined how much bigger a limb should be, compared to the other normal limb, before a diagnosis of lymphoedema can be made.

Devices that measure moisture under the skin have been marketed as a non-invasive way of diagnosing lymphoedema, but studies have shown that they are not reliable.

We use Indocyanine Green (ICG) lymphography to detect lymphoedema in the earliest phases of disease. This technique is very similar to lymphoscintigraphy, but it shows the lymph vessels in a small area rather than a whole limb, which means the individual vessels can be seen much more clearly. A tiny amount of green dye is injected into the wrist or the foot which is taken up by the lymph system, allowing the functioning lymph vessels to be located and mapped, and showing any abnormal patterns. Not only does this scan allow a definitive diagnosis of lymphoedema to be made, but it also identifies which are the functioning lymph vessels that can then be used for reconstructive surgery (see page 108).

RAISING AWARENESS

Clearly, the lack of awareness surrounding lymphoedema is a problem that affects both patients and doctors. Medic, author, television presenter and journalist Dr Miriam Stoppard considers how the condition can be given the attention it needs and deserves:

In medicine we have a family of conditions that are given little attention – even ignored – that don't excite, that are often dismissed as unworthy of attention and are universally overlooked and neglected.

We call them the Cinderellas of medicine, and they include lymphoedema, fibromyalgia, family medicine, palliative care, geriatrics, my own speciality dermatology and sexual health. They are underappreciated, under discussed and underfunded, and woe betide any patient who suffers from one. They may find that their doctor is unaware of its existence and even if they are, give it low priority.

As Dr Jonathan Moore says (see page 56), this is partly because these Cinderellas are given little prominence during medical training and so they remain mysterious, on the edges of medical knowledge.

And, dare I say it, one of the reasons that lymphoedema is so under-served is that, in the main, it's a woman's complaint. I don't think there's a single condition where the female form of the disease has as high a profile as the male form. For decades all the research into heart disease was done in men. Ditto lung cancer. Until we rate female complaints as important as male ones we can't correct this bias, and lymphoedema sufferers will continue to be neglected.

Now, if lymphoedema is seen as a Cinderella condition by the medical profession, it really is beneath the salt as far as the media is concerned, especially tabloid journalism where I work. My editor demands 'sexy' and lymphoedema assuredly isn't.

I feel there are two aspects of lymphoedema that could raise its profile in the media: the first is in the hands of cancer surgeons. Yes, I know nailing the cancer and its spread is the primary aim and no surgeon can be blamed for focussing on survival stats. But as both breast cancer and ovarian cancer involve removal or destruction of lymph nodes, distorting lymphatic anatomy and curbing drainage, the chance of lymphoedema is high. Surely it behoves all surgeons (and hopefully all doctors) to keep lymphoedema firmly in their sights, publicise its treatment and management, and give priority to working alongside lymphoedema experts, doctors and nurses. It needs a high profile and shouldn't be buried in a list of unwanted complications. Specialist therapists and breast care nurses are essential to the treatments. Doctors should be in the forefront of publicising this.

The other aspect of lymphoedema that makes good copy (and I've written about it several times in my paper during the last two years) is advances in treatment and management. My readers, and most viewers I reckon, are keenly tuned in to the promise of new and better treatments. Lymphoedema is no exception, especially as it's likely to afflict up to a quarter of women in the year after breast cancer surgery, depending on the number of lymph nodes removed, and will persist long into the future, especially if local radiation follows surgery.

There's much demystifying to be done and myths to be busted. 'Upper body exercise promotes lymphoedema among breast cancer survivors.' No, it doesn't. 'Nothing can be done for lymphoedema.' Wrong, much can. 'I can't lift anything or be active any more.' Untrue, you can be active and strong again.

There's a lot of good news about lymphoedema but the media won't come to meet lymphoedema sufferers without a 'hook'. The key is case histories. The media love case histories. You'd be surprised how many takers there'd be for an upbeat press release larded with uplifting case studies; and how about a poster for GPs' surgeries to raise awareness for both doctors and patients?

Raising awareness and increasing the amount of research into lymphoedema won't happen overnight, but this is something that needs our attention. If we can make this condition a more mainstream concern, perhaps we can make real progress towards finding a cure. Until that time, though, there are ways of managing the disease and treating the symptoms.

7

Standard Treatments

As a rule, doctors rely on the use of a drug or an operation to treat most medical conditions, but there is currently no drug therapy for lymphoedema and surgery works for only certain types of swelling. Consequently most doctors say that there is no treatment for the condition, but this nihilistic approach to lymphoedema is unfair. While we have to accept that, at present, there is no outright cure for the condition, there are certainly effective treatments available to alleviate the symptoms. First, though, let's deal with two regularly suggested treatments that are known not to be especially effective.

It is standard practice to tell anyone with a swollen foot or ankle to elevate the legs to get the swelling to go down. In general this does help reduce all types of oedema as it collapses the veins so that the fluid flow into the tissues is reduced and the lymph system can catch up and drain the fluid away. But elevating the legs doesn't improve lymph drainage itself, so it is much less effective in cases of lymphoedema. An ankle that has swollen due to varicose veins will usually resolve completely overnight, however an ankle swollen from lymphoedema will only reduce by an average of 10 per cent.

Another ploy is to give diuretics, but these aren't effective in cases of lymphoedema either. What diuretics do is remove fluid from the body via the kidneys; they have no effect on lymph drainage. When given to a patient with lymphoedema, they may lead to a slight reduction in swelling, but only because there is less water in the body overall.

These methods apart, there are a number of effective ways to manage lymphoedema. They fall into four main categories: exercise and physical therapy, manual lymphatic drainage, compression and skin care.

EXERCISE AND PHYSICAL THERAPY

As we've seen, exercise is key to encouraging lymph drainage (see page 8), and so is one of the most important areas of management. The problem is that lymphoedema sufferers tend to experience loss of flexibility, stiffness and reduced mobility as part of their condition, which obviously makes it more difficult to be active. One patient, Mark, tells his story:

I turned forty in January 2011 and it started very well indeed; the launch of my first new business venture, happily married, two beautiful daughters and not a grey hair in sight! On Father's Day that year though, I became very poorly, very quickly. It transpired I had cellulitis. After thirteen long days in hospital, the infection was under control, but a new challenge had arisen. I now had lymphoedema, which affected the whole of my left leg. Intensive lymphoedema treatment and regular wearing of my strong compression stocking has successfully reduced the size of my left leg but it is still bigger than my right.

More recently I have endured constant and frequently excruciating pain in both hips, my right leg and lower back, which has made it difficult to walk any distance. I am told it is the lymphoedema that has caused this because I tend to swing the heavy leg when I walk, which has strained my back. Exercise is widely recommended as treatment, but that isn't easy for me – even trying to get through a round of golf, my hips feel as though bone is rubbing on bone. Walking uphill, I feel like I'm in my eighties not forties and getting up after sitting for a while is a three-stage process to get totally upright. I am now under weekly physiotherapy treatments to try and improve the situation.

It's particularly important to address problems with balance and gait as these can lead to accidents. Also, a patient with a heavy, swollen leg might drag it behind or swing it outwards in an arc, which can strain other parts of the body, especially the back. Physiotherapy aims to reduce these sorts of problems by ensuring good posture, strengthening core muscles and teaching as normal a style of walking as possible.

Marie-Clare Johnson is a physiotherapist and shoulder specialist, and she is well aware how important physiotherapy can be in helping patients regain a normal range of movement:

Some of the specific challenges that lymphoedema brings include heaviness, aching, reduced mobility and range of movement, balance issues and reduced strength. All of these problems can be helped through physiotherapy.

Physiotherapists can devise a tailored exercise programme that will help patients gain strength, relieve some of the fatigue and weakness they often experience, and generally help to clear the fluid. Stretching and mobilising sore, tight tissues is so important and can easily be incorporated into people's lives. Such exercises can help patients to perform simple, everyday activities such as reaching into high cupboards or putting on clothes as well as more energetic pursuits such as tennis.

Conditions such as lymphoedema can also change the body's shape, which in turn can affect movement. Sometimes a patient needs to learn how to move in a new and unfamiliar way to compensate for this, which can feel strange and unnatural at first, so it is so important to find a way to build it in to your daily life.

Once patients learn how to make simple movements again, they are more prepared for a fuller exercise pro-gramme, which is so important to minimise the impact of lymphoedema, as well as improve confidence, independ-ence, strength and quality of life.

One of Marie-Clare's patients, Anne, knows from first-hand expe-rience just how beneficial physiotherapy can be as a preparation for a broader exercise regime:

I had been completely fit and healthy until I got breast cancer. I had a full-time job as a secretary, looked after the home, took the dogs out for a walk each day and still managed to play tennis twice a week.

I sailed through my surgery, chemo and radiotherapy. I am right handed, and that was the side of the lymph gland removal, so I was careful to protect my right arm. One day, however, I stretched to reach an item in a high cupboard and felt something pull under my arm. I did not think any-thing of it until two days later I noticed my arm was slightly swollen. It did not really hurt but ached, and using it was more difficult. I was nervous of holding on to the dog lead with my right arm and it was looking increasingly unlikely I would get back to tennis.

However I was referred for physiotherapy and after a series of treatments my arm started to feel a lot better. The therapist said my shoulder had stiffened. A series of gentle stretching exercises has helped the range of movement so there is no longer any discomfort. I was also given some strengthening, or what was called resistance exercises, because she said the muscles of the arm had become weak. I was also recommended to do aqua aerobics and light swimming. The exercises have made a big difference in what I can now do, and the swelling has also improved. I have even returned to playing tennis cautiously.

Traditionally, those at risk of lymphoedema have been advised to 'protect' the affected limb, but more recent evidence indicates that exercising it can be much more beneficial – a progressive weight-lifting programme in women following breast cancer treatment, for example, may help reduce the incidence of lymphoedema. Building strength in this way should mean that the arm will better withstand strains that are part of everyday life, such as reaching up for a top shelf or carrying heavy shopping. Upper body exercise should start at a very low intensity and progress slowly and according to how the arm feels in order to gradually increase strength.

Of course, while physiotherapy and exercise are very important, they can be difficult if you have very painful limbs. In this case you may need a specially designed exercise programme tailored to suit your own needs and abilities. Jon Bowskill is a remedial exercise specialist who does just that (see Appendix 1). He has a number of tips for incorporating exercise into daily life in achievable ways:

Exercise for lymphoedema can be done in many ways, but perhaps the most easy and accessible is simply to incorporate it into your everyday tasks. Perhaps you could:

- Get off the tube or bus one stop early
- Take the stairs instead of lift or escalators
- Take time out of your day for a brisk walk at lunchtime
- Try to swing your arms and breathe deeply as you walk
- Alter your home cleaning routines to make them more challenging
- Take a few minutes each day for some gentle yoga or tai chi
- Practise diaphragmatic breathing or tummy breathing before bed and regularly through the day
- Use a smart phone app to measure how far you walk each day
- Try, when sitting, to move the wrists, ankles, shoulders and elbows in gentle circles to aid circulation

As a general rule you should work to elevate your heart rate to a level where you can feel your breathing rate increase, but only to the stage where you could comfortably still hold a conversation. On a scale of 1–10 (10 being exhausting, and zero being no effort at all), this should fit somewhere between 3–5.

When we sleep well, drink plenty of water, eat a good diet (for advice on nutrition see Appendix 2, page 197) and are free from stress, illness and disease, our bodies can cope with quite a lot of exercise and at a relatively high intensity. But the more stress and strain the body is under, the more difficult it is to recover from strenuous exercise and it can actually have a negative effect on your health, despite the best intentions.

With lymphoedema, finding the correct intensity and form of exercise for your level of well-being is crucial to make sure your efforts are helping your condition. Gently experiment with any activity and let your body tell you what it does and doesn't like, adjusting what you are doing accordingly. It's also worth taking these five precautions:

1. Avoid staying too long in a static position
2. Avoid anything that forces you to grip too firmly for long periods
3. If you have upper body swelling be careful of strenuous upper body gym work unless under the guidance of a lymphoedema physiotherapist
4. Make sure that where possible you wear your compression garments for exercising
5. Make sure that you stretch to warm up and cool down

MANUAL LYMPH DRAINAGE

Manual lymph drainage (MLD) is a treatment that involves massaging the tissues through specific hand movements on the skin surface to encourage lymph drainage. The specific hand movements vary between the different schools of massage (these include names like Vodder, Foeldi, Le Duc and Casley-Smith) but the objective is the same, namely to direct lymph flow away from congested areas of lymph to parts of the body where drainage is working more effectively.

Whatever school of massage you are advised to follow, the hand movements are gentle but firm on the skin. There is no rubbing or friction. The idea is to gently stimulate fluid to enter the smaller lymph vessels and then drain away, like a siphoning effect, improving the flow of lymph in the affected region.

MLD is most useful at sites of lymph congestion where compression and exercise cannot be applied. For example, in arm lymphoedema, congestion may occur around the shoulder, above the point that a compression sleeve or bandage can reach. By decongesting the shoulder area lymph can subsequently drain more freely from the rest of the arm. Parts of the body that fall in the central line between the head and the genital area (such as the neck, breast, torso, and the head and genital area themselves) particularly benefit from MLD because it is more difficult to treat them with exercise and compression techniques.

Mark Pearson is an MLD therapist who witnesses the beneficial effects of the technique on a daily basis:

My background is sports massage, which mostly involves deep tissue massages on rugby players and the like. Lymphoedema was only lightly covered in my basic training and was left as a specialism for postgraduate level. However, one day I started working at a local hospice, and palliative care soon became a passion of mine.

It was at the hospice that I first met a patient with lymphoedema in her arm – a delightful little eighty-three-

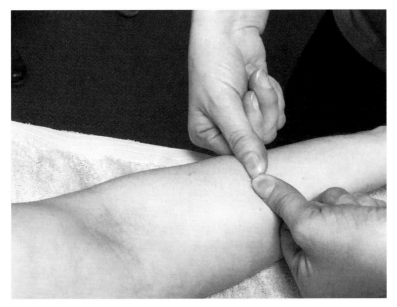

Lymphatic massage, known as MLD, involves gentle repetitive hand movements on the skin to encourage lymph fluid to drain in one direction.

year-old lady, who walked in with an arm bigger than my leg. The weight of the arm was causing her to stoop and as she heaved it onto the couch, she stoically remarked that her knees weren't what they used to be, but wasn't it a lovely day . . .

I remember thinking 'And what am I going to do next?' But there was no formal lymphoedema service at the hospice so, with my limited knowledge, I started to massage the arm. I used the lightest touch on her woody, brawny arm and she sank into a state of relaxation. Twenty minutes later she thought I was some kind of deity and advocated my skills vocally in the unit as she left.

But I wasn't happy. I didn't know what lymphoedema really was, nor how I could help make it better, so after making some enquiries, I sought out the Vodder School and embarked on becoming a MLD therapist.

After two training courses, off I went into the world with my new qualification. A few weeks later the phone rang and a nurse from a hospital in London asked if I could make a house call to assess and treat a seriously overweight patient.

The treatment was for six weeks. I had to do daily MLD, sometimes followed by bandaging on both legs (the MLD siphons the lymph away from the swollen area while the bandaging helps to squeeze it along), until the patient was ready to transfer into compression hosiery. At first I have to admit I was not convinced the MLD was doing any good. One day I suggested to the patient that we cut the MLD as surely the bandages were doing the trick. I was met with sheer indignation: 'I think not young man. After you leave I have to use two bed pans it moves so much fluid – you keep MLD'ing and I'll keep weeing!' I realised my treatment was making a difference.

Back at the hospice things were fast moving on as more and more patients were referred to me both in the clinic and on the wards, as staff started getting positive feedback from patients I had treated with MLD. My knowledge and understanding of the lymph system was increasing.

I got a job at St George's Hospital in Tooting and was soon getting all the chronic swelling cases in the area. One lady had bilateral lower limb swelling after cancer: 'Now then all I want is that massage you do. I don't want bandages. I don't want tights. I'm tired . . . and I want massage,' was her opening remark. After three sessions of MLD I persuaded her to add in the bandaging from toe to groin on both legs. Her legs responded beautifully and after two weeks she transferred to a pair of light compression tights.

My practice expanded, but I started to realise the lack of knowledge and provision of care amongst doctors and community staff means that lymphoedema sufferers have to source their own treatment. MLD therapists are a good first port of call as it is often we who provide most information and initial treatment for lymphoedema. However, although some of us may be accessible through the NHS (usually through a hospice), that is rare and the majority of us work privately. Most patients would like to have MLD frequently as part of a long-term treatment, but as money within healthcare becomes ever more scarce, so the use of MLD is best targeted to those who benefit most. It is particularly helpful for intensive periods of treatment and for midline lymphoedema (the face, head and neck, breast, torso and genitalia).

There is nothing to stop anyone having MLD privately, but it may not prove cost effective. MLD is a highly skilled and labour intensive treatment technique, but a version of MLD called simple lymphatic drainage (SLD) can be taught so the patient themselves, or partner, or carer can perform it.

COMPRESSION

Exercise is very beneficial as we've seen, but what really stimulates lymph drainage is muscle contraction alongside compression. Exercising a limb encased in a bandage or compression garment increases the pressure within the tissues during the muscle contraction and helps to 'squeeze' the tissues, encouraging lymph drainage.

Exercising in water can have the same effect because the water provides the compression and the exercise works the muscles. The deeper the water the greater the pressure on the skin and the greater the massaging effect on the swollen tissues.

Bandaging

Compression therapy comes in different forms, but bandaging is particularly effective for treating severe cases of lymphoedema. Sue Lawrance, a lymphoedema therapist, and Lynn Finch, who works with lymphoedema treatment products, explain why it's beneficial to use bandaging:

> Leg bandaging has been used for centuries to reduce swelling and heal wounds. The pressure generated is much higher than compression garments as the latter are made to fit a normal-shaped limb, and so the more swollen or misshapen the limb, the more uneven the pressure applied by the garment. Also, the bigger the circumference of a leg (or arm), the more difficult it is to apply sufficient pressure to reduce swelling. Therefore bandages are usually more effective at reducing swelling and improving general limb shape, to the point that patients can then start using a compression garment, which will then be more effective at controlling the swelling longer term. It has not been unknown for patients to return to clinic carrying a perfectly formed bandage (but without their arm in it) because it had 'simply fallen off in bed' when they rolled over, the arm having shrunk so much from the compression.

The bandage helps to reduce the swelling because when a muscle expands during exercise, it pushes against the rigid binding, encouraging lymph drainage. So it is very important to exercise when wearing the bandages; otherwise lymph drainage is not being stimulated. The bandages also help to prevent fluid from flowing back into the limb after exercise, and because the bandages are non-elastic, when the limb is elevated and at rest, the pressure reduces, providing comfortable support rather than continuing to squeeze the muscles.

Bandaging is also the best way to reverse skin changes – the skin can become thicker and harder, as do the tissues immediately beneath the skin, which can prevent compression garments from working properly. Sometimes the pressure of fluid within the swollen skin is so great that lymph 'leaks' through the skin. Not only will it wet clothing and bedding, it poses an infection risk, and bandaging is the main way to reverse the leaking.

HOW MULTI-LAYER BANDAGING WORKS

Applying multiple layers of bandage, one on top of the other, achieves a more rigid and more secure effect, as the bandages are less likely to unravel. The short-stretch bandages are non-elasticated, which also helps give a firm structure. The layers are made up of a soft tubular cotton bandage next to the skin, then cotton padding on top, which is used to iron out any dips in the skin surface contour, and then a strong cotton bandage as the top layer.

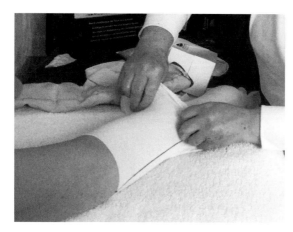

Preparing the hand and arm for compression bandaging with a soft cotton bandage to protect the skin, for a patient who developed lymphoedema after an episode of cellulitis caused by a cat's bite.

The bandaging of the hand and arm starts with the fingers.

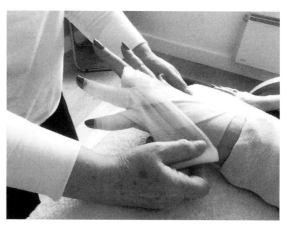

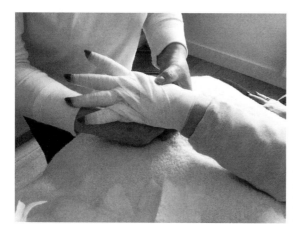

Each finger is carefully bandaged individually to encourage lymph drainage along the entire limb, from the tips all the way up the arm.

Once the fingers and hand have been bandaged, padding is applied to the palm and then the top of the hand, to deal with stubborn lymphoedemous areas of the hand.

Finally, additional soft padding is applied over the hand and arm, which makes it all much bulkier but also makes it more comfortable for the patient. Bandages are then firmly applied.

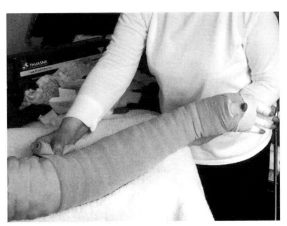

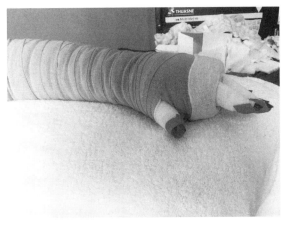

The bandages will be kept on for twenty-four hours, during which time patients are also encouraged to do some gentle exercises to help achieve the best possible results.

A severely swollen lymphoedema limb forms skin folds that bulge out. Flattening these folds is essential before fitting garments and the key to this is a correctly applied second layer of padding. It's important not to overuse padding because it can make the overall pressure less effective.

Bandaging also only works effectively if it is applied to a limb that is cylindrical in shape. The more misshapen a limb is, the more difficult it is to apply an even pressure around the limb. So hands and feet are trickier to bandage than a 'round' leg; you end up with higher pressure on the sides than the top of the foot or hand. Cotton padding is designed to iron out the unevenness of the limb shape with the strongest bandages applied on top of it. Hence, more padding is put on top of a foot so the shape is more rounded.

Traditionally, bandages have always been applied from the base of the toes to just below the knee. This is the way community nurses are usually trained to do it, but although this may work well to heal leg ulcers or control skin problems from varicose veins, in lymphoedema this approach can actually make the swelling worse. The toes can become even more sausage shaped and swelling can increase around the knee causing stiffness of the joint and limited movement. Therefore multi-layer lymphoedema bandaging should always include bandaging of the toes while extending the bandaging over the knees and up to the groin.

HOW LONG DO YOU NEED BANDAGES?

Bandages should be worn over a period of anything between one to four weeks – or possibly more in some instances, depending on the severity of the swelling. They should be replaced every twenty-four to forty-eight hours – they stay on overnight to discourage the fluid from coming back.

Bandages can be bulky and cumbersome, so some patients initially resist the idea of wearing them continuously for twenty-four hours because of the adjustments needed for everyday tasks – washing, wearing normal shoes, etc. – but seeing the results once the bandages are removed can encourage patients to continue whatever the inconvenience caused.

TRANSFERRING TO COMPRESSION GARMENTS

Once the bandaging phase has finished, the patient needs to immediately switch to a compression garment. The transfer needs to be seamless, as if there is a gap between the two, the limb will soon swell again and most of the hard work to get to this point will have been in vain. So the therapist should measure for the best-fitted garment at the point when the bandaging is no longer reducing the swelling. The garment should be ordered and the bandaging continued until the garment is available to wear.

Decongestive lymphatic therapy

Decongestive lymphatic therapy (DLT) is when MLD is used in combination with exercise and compression bandaging in intensive lymphoedema treatment. DLT is also sometimes called CDT (complete decongestive therapy), but there is nothing in that name to indicate it is used to treat the lymph system, and there is confusion as to what the C stands for (complete, combined and complex are often used interchangeably), so DLT is the preferred term.

DLT is carried out daily (or sometimes every second or third day). MLD is performed first to decongest the areas and improve lymph flow. Then, bandages are applied and exercise encouraged.

The purpose of an intensive course of treatment is to improve the size and shape of a swollen limb as quickly as possible so that the subsequent maintenance treatment with compression garments is more effective. Mild cases of lymphoedema do not usually need DLT because compression garments can be made to fit. In the case of large limbs, or where the shape will not allow the fitting of a compression garment, then DLT is used first.

DLT is also used in circumstances where the skin is problematic, for example, if it has become very thickened or hardened; it may be nobbly, like cobblestone, or very warty on the surface; lymph may be leaking through the skin or there may be a chronic wound. In all these circumstances DLT would be used to reverse these abnormalities before a compression garment can be fitted.

Compression garments

A compression garment is a piece of elastic fabric, fitted to the outside of a body part, providing external pressure and conforming to the shape of the limb. A range of compression items can be used to treat lymphoedema, so you will sometimes hear references to stockings, hosiery, pantyhose, tights and sleeves, but 'garment' is probably the best catch-all term.

Let's admit defeat on certain aspects of wearing compression garments. Yes, they are difficult to get on and off; yes, they are thicker than a sheer 7-denier stocking, and yes, they can be hot during summer – but there are benefits! They really can improve circulation both in the veins and in the lymph system of the affected area.

A compression garment is designed to match the shape of the limb, and to apply comfortable pressure. There must be a gradient of compression, with higher pressure applied at the extremities of the limb, and slowly reducing pressure towards the trunk of the body. This gradient tries to mirror the pressure of water when standing waist deep in a swimming pool. It is designed to encourage blood and lymph to drain upwards against the forces of gravity. A stocking that does this is called a graduated compression stocking. If the pressure were higher at the top rather than the bottom of a stocking then blood and lymph flow would be obstructed.

There are lots of different types of compression garment available, but not all of them will be suitable. Most of the readily available garments only provide light pressure, which isn't enough to have a beneficial effect on a limb swollen by lymphoedema. The white stockings often worn in hospital, known as anti-thrombotic or anti-embolism or thrombo-embolic deterrent (TED) stockings; flight or travel socks; compression sportswear; and support stockings are generally not suitable for sufferers of lymphoedema. They can help prevent DVT or control mild oedema, but most are not built to last and deteriorate after a few washes, whereas compression stockings for lymphoedema are more robust and can be expected to last as long as six months. So it is important to make sure you are wearing the correct compression garment for you.

Types of compression garment

There are all sorts of compression garment, in different strengths, sizes, materials and colours. They can be custom-made or bought off the shelf, and they're made for different parts of the body: a stocking usually either stops just below the knee ('knee-high') or just below the groin ('thigh-high'); garments can be open or close-toed; pantyhose (or tights) enclose the lower trunk; an anklet is a sock that reaches just above the ankle; toe gloves fit over the toes and reach usually to mid-foot; a sleeve extends from wrist to armpit; gloves enclose the hand and fingers and some sleeves can have a glove attached. There are also made-to-measure garments designed to treat other regions affected by lymphoedema, such as the breast, torso and genitalia.

All of these garments can come in two types, depending on the knitting process used. Circular-knit stockings are made without seams. People tend to prefer the look of these garments, but they are stretchier and generally only offer a light compression, so are used for varicose veins and milder forms of lymphoedema. Flat-knitted stockings are knitted stitch by stitch to follow precisely the contours of the afflicted area. The fabric is then sewn together with a flat, elastic seam. The thicker fabric offers a massaging effect, which promotes lymph drainage, and is stronger, which ensures the stocking does not yield to the oedema.

As with buying suits, compression garments can be 'off the shelf' or 'made to measure'. Off-the-shelf garments come in set sizes whereas made-to-measure are fitted exactly to a person's body.

Compression strengths

Compression stockings come in different strengths referred to as compression classes. Class I provides light compression, class II provides medium compression, class III provides high compression and class IV provides very high compression (the precise pressures these classes exert differ from one country to another). Light compression is usually used for mild oedema and very high compression prescribed for severe lymphoedema.

For most cases of lymphoedema, except mild swelling, it is sensible to consult a professional experienced and trained in the use of compression garments in order to get yourself measured for the best garment. It is very important to get the right strength as, if it isn't tight enough, it won't have any effect, but if it's too tight, it risks cutting off the blood circulation, particularly if your circulation is poor to begin with (which can be often be the case for the elderly).

Flat-knit garments, for more severe cases, are prescription only. Lower compression garments might be prescribed but can also be bought without a prescription, providing you know your size. Pharmacists are trained to fit and provide over-the-counter compression garments, so your local pharmacy can be a good place to start.

Compression garments need to be looked after well if they are to last their expected life span of six months. You should get two pairs, one to wear and one to wash. Each garment needs to be washed after a day's wear in order to retain its elasticity. Hand-washing is best because heat from a washing machine can damage the fabric. You should also avoid using conditioner or drying the garment on a radiator for the same reason.

Wearing the garments

It can be difficult to get the garments on and off at first, so it is important to get proper instruction. Turning stockings and sleeves inside-out in order to put them on is not a good idea because they are twice as difficult to stretch when doubled over. It's also important not to yank the garment on, as it can overstretch the fabric. Easing them on a bit at a time is the best way. It can help to wear disposable or rubber gloves as they give you a better grip. Sleeves and stockings should be fitted to exactly the right length and never doubled over at the top if they are too long as that will create the same effect as an elastic band – sharply increasing the pressure around that portion of the limb, stifling the flow of lymph and blood.

Posture is also important, especially when putting on stockings, as it can easily lead to lower back pain. For those of us with arthritis, or with too big a tummy to reach down to our feet, various aids for application can be purchased.

Sleeves and stockings are designed to work when moving, so they would normally be removed when going to bed and put back on in the morning, unless the doctor or therapist has advised otherwise.

A manufacturer's view

There are lots of different options for compression garments; Annerose Zorn and Juergen Gold of the stocking manufacturer Juzo share their experience of producing these garments:

Juzo (Julius Zorn GMBH) is a family-owned global company, which has been providing solutions to the problems faced by lymphoedema patients, among others, since 1912. Working from our factory in Germany, we offer a range of garments for the whole body, both flat- and circular-knitted, produced in a myriad of shapes, sizes and colours, with over 17,000 items on prescription in the UK, as well a full range of aids and accessories.

Garments have to go through many processes in order to be made – even off-the-shelf garments have to pass through at least eight processes before they get to the patient. Some of the made-to-measure garments – the best choice for more severe cases of lymphoedema – can have over fifty processes in order to make them fit perfectly!

Over the years we have seen many innovations from all the compression garment manufacturers, and Juzo is no exception. On a Juzo garment the seam is one stitch wide, which means it sits flat when the garment is worn to make it more comfortable – and the seam is also hand-rolled to make it even flatter. All garments are hand-checked at least five times. We are the first manufacturer to offer not only advanced comfort but also trendy colours in flat-knitted garments: we have a softer flat-knit in a class IV garment, a flat-knitted face mask with only one seam, and over sixteen colours as well as tie-dye options. We are also the first to offer lymphoedema garments for animals and we have introduced a training academy to help spread our knowledge and expertise.

We are always introducing new processes that enable us to continue to make highly effective garments, but, most importantly, we care about our customers and always listen to them to find out how we can make our

A knitting expert checking the workings of a circular-knit knitting machine.

A body/thorax compression garment with integral breast cup undergoing tests in the garment testing room.

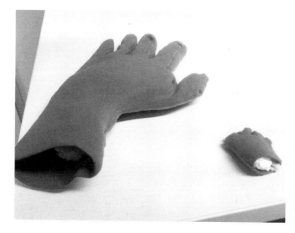

Lymphoedema can affect people of all ages – but help is always available from Juzo. Here an adult glove and a glove for a nine month old.

A made-to-measure garment coming off the knitting machine.

Every made-to-measure (and standard) garment is hand checked several times.

Even animals can suffer from lymphoedema – this is a specially made product for a horse.

garments more appealing to them. We are always working towards making garments easier to live with, easier to get on and off, easier to care for and more attractive. After all, it was our founder Julius Zorn who said, 'Helping is our life's work'.

Compression garments might seem a tiresome effort, but they really can make all the difference. And being able to manage the swelling properly is so important – not only can it allow patients to get on with their lives as normally as possible, it stops the problem from getting out of hand, as Janet discovered:

One evening while on holiday with my family I put on a little cardigan and noticed that my right arm simply wouldn't fit into the sleeve. I knew straight away that I was facing another consequence of breast cancer – a very visible effect that I would be unable to hide each day as I could with my flat chest.

In the grand scheme of what I had been through over eleven years of cancer (two lumpectomies, eventual double mastectomy, two radiotherapy cycles and three chemotherapy treatments) this should have been minor, but I found it so devastating. For the first few years I tried to ignore it, hoping it would just go away. I ordered my own sleeves from the internet (guessing at my measurements) and wore them only occasionally – mostly when I exercised but rarely at any other time. Once or twice I saw a massage therapist (not a certified lymphoedema specialist) and simply asked them to massage my arm in any way that they felt would assist. My arm got worse and worse.

Finally I went to see my lymphoedema therapist. I sat on her treatment bed and showed her my arm and my sleeves and told her just a little bit about myself – and as I did I realised that tears were quietly falling onto my lap and all I could think of was how cross I was with myself because I hadn't cried for ages. She gently felt my arm; she took loads of measurements; she looked at my tattered sleeves and told me to throw them all away. She said she was impressed with how well I had managed it on my own, but told me in no uncertain terms that if I didn't sort it out soon then it was only going to get worse.

I had gone to that appointment intending it to be just a one-off visit – I had neither the time nor inclination to see someone regularly, and was convinced I was doing just fine on my own. Yet two months later I have been to see her virtually every week. I have three new sleeves – all properly measured – and the tools to manage my lymphoedema effectively. As a result my arm is heaps better.

SKIN CARE

As explained earlier, lymphoedema can cause your skin to grow thicker and stiffer. The less malleable your skin is, the more likely it is to break, so germs are much more likely to get into the cracks and crevices, increasing the risk of cellulitis. The thickened skin can also limit the range of your joint movement, which can be uncomfortable and affect mobility. Reversing these skin changes is therefore a very important part of lymphoedema treatment.

As with the treatment of any skin disease, moisturisers, also known as emollients, are used to rehydrate the skin. This is essential to help your skin perform one of its most important functions – that of acting as an effective barrier, holding vital fluids in, and keeping germs and toxins out. They can also soften and remove the scales and debris that build up on dry skin. Most people prefer cream-based moisturiers as they are more pleasant to use but oils and greases (for example, white soft paraffin, like Vaseline), are actually the most effective for lymphoedema.

Washing is also an important way to minimise the amount of bacteria on your skin. You can do this with soap, but that can dry out the skin so a cream, used as a soap substitute, will work just as well while at the same time keeping your skin hydrated.

These two simple steps – washing and moisturising – can make all the difference, not only improving the quality of the skin but also reducing cases of infection. The value of skin care in lymph-oedema is no better illustrated than in the treatment of filarial lymphoedema and podoconiosis (see Chapter 13).

Foot care

Lymphoedema can have a particularly debilitating effect on your feet, requiring specific attention to counteract it. Nigel Tewkesbury, a podiatrist, describes the difficulties people with swollen feet en-counter and how podiatrists can help:

As a young podiatrist, some forty years ago, I remember well my first encounter with lymphoedema. I was on a home visit to a woman, whom I found sitting in an armchair, with her huge swollen legs supported by a cushioned stool. Her limbs were not only red and enlarged but they also had blisters on them and the skin was leaking fluid onto a thick towel. She was unable to walk easily and had become, effectively, a prisoner in her flat. It made a huge impression on me.

As a podiatrist it is my role, along with diagnosing and treating a wide range of foot problems, to improve mobility, independence and quality of life for my patients. When it comes to lymphoedema, which we encounter all too frequently, the action of walking greatly assists the removal of fluid in the legs and wearing suitable shoes is very important.

Foot lymphoedema creates a number of problems; in hot climates foot swelling can reach gigantic proportions so that no shoes fit and the skin is fit to burst. The only choice for footwear in these circumstances is sandals, which can make the swelling even worse, and it can become painful and tender. Walking can become difficult, with or without footwear, which can then cause problems with balance, making a fall more likely.

One of the biggest problems, however, is infection, which can be very common in foot lymphoedema. Lymphoedema produces a marked thickening of the skin, particularly over the forefoot, as well as thicker toenails, and such unhealthy skin harbours more germs that can lead to infection.

People with lymphoedema also live in fear of insect bites, not only because the inflammatory reaction is often severe leading to worse pain and swelling, but also because of the high risk of cellulitis.

The most frequent infection, though, is fungal – it's made almost inevitable by the close contact between swollen toes leading to a moist warm environment ideally suited to fungus. Careful drying between the toes, plus the use of an alcohol wipe now and again can reduce skin maceration and irritation. Any disturbance to the skin integrity between the toes increases the risk of infections considerably. Toenails are also more likely to be infected with fungus. So skin care is very important for managing foot lymphoedema.

Other problems related to foot lymphoedema are the bulging nail-folds of swollen toes which often lead to ingrowing toenails, particularly in infants and young children. Therefore careful cutting of toenails is extremely important at all ages. Viral warts or verrucas are also not only more likely but also more difficult to get rid of, again because of the reduced immune response of the local tissues to infection; and corns and calluses often develop because of the tight fitting of shoes when swelling increases, and from the effect of ill-fitting compression garments.

Choosing the right shoes can be a key part of controlling the swelling – a lace-up shoe or boot, for example, provides helpful compression (providing the shoe can be got on in the first place), while slippers, open-toed sandals with thong or even a court shoe can exacerbate the swelling.

Inevitably, the choice of footwear may be somewhat limited due to the swelling (shoes are not routinely built to accommodate a domed bulge on top of the foot) and rarely do high-street shoe shops offer suitable options. There is, however, a wide network of small independent shoe retail shops owned by people passionate about fitting shoes for

A swollen foot causes immense problems with footwear. The shape of the shoe is often stretched and distorted, which in turn reduces the shoe's support function, making a normal gait more difficult, and further affecting lymph drainage.

wider or swollen feet. These specialist footwear outlets can be accessed in the UK through the patients' organisation the Lymphoedema Support Network.

Podiatrists, I believe, have an important role to play in the management of lymphoedema. We often see our patients on a regular basis, and they develop confidence in us and frequently seek our advice on health matters. We maintain their feet in optimum condition and strive to keep them free from bacterial and fungal infections. And because patients tend to have to expose their lower limbs during a foot examination, we can also help with any skin lesions on their legs. We must be ready to refer our patients to lymphoedema support groups and lymphoedema specialists to enable them to receive the very best help in diagnosis and management of this very distressing condition.

These are the standard ways of managing lymphoedema. They may at times seem tiresome, requiring considerable and constant effort for not much reward. However, these days there are some other options that may also be effective, as progress is made in new and innovative treatments.

8

New and Alternative Treatments

T he standard treatment options for lymphoedema are effective, but they can be time-consuming and require a lot of effort. Doctors and patients alike are always keen to find out more about innovative ways to treat or manage lymphoedema, especially if it can make life a bit easier for the patient.

INNOVATIVE PRODUCTS

Jane Wigg, one of the most experienced lymphoedema therapists in the UK, is constantly looking for new ways to tackle the condition:

I have been working in the field of lymphoedema for over twenty years. What I hope for one day is a future where garments are consigned to the history books and where people living with lymphoedema will have an easier way of life. I am always on the lookout for treatments and solutions that bring us closer to that day.

People come to me with new products because they know I'm willing to take a look, be open-minded and implement them if they work. My patients have had all the latest gadgets tried out on them that measure, diagnose, pump, drain, squash or suck . . . we've tried them all. Here are some of the latest innovations that really can make a difference:

MEASURING LYMPHOEDEMA

If you came to our clinic, we would most likely measure the swelling with a Perometer, rather than a traditional tape measure. You put your arm or leg inside the frame of the machine, and it uses a series of harmless light beams to make an accurate measurement.

We also employ a technique called tissue dielectric constant (TDC), which uses a small electrode to send a harmless electrical current through the skin, allowing us to measure the body's fluid composition. It is good for detecting early lymphoedema in arms and legs but it is particularly helpful for measuring swelling in the breast, head and neck or genitals, where a tape measure is difficult to use.

SEEING LYMPH VESSELS WORK

We use ICG lymphography to map the lymph drainage routes (see page 63). It can also help with treatments such as MLD, and to assess who might be suitable for microsurgery (see page 108). Based on this technology, together with Professor Belgrado from Brussels, we have also introduced a technique called Fluoroscopy Guided Manual Lymphatic Drainage (FG-MLD) that allows us to see what hand movements are required to 'fill' the lymph vessels and 'flush' the fluid away.

COMPRESSION ALTERNATIVES

If you can't wear a compression garment for whatever reason then we might recommend a Velcro wrap device. This is

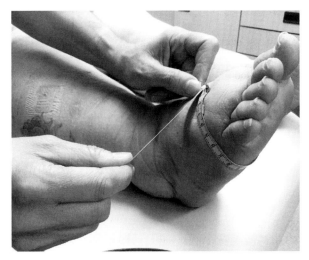

The severity of the swelling in a limb can be measured either by hand using a tape measure or with a machine such as a Perometer. The Perometer has as series of lights within a frame. The frame is moved up and down the limb and the lights shine on the skin so recording the circumference at multiple points up the limb. In this way volume can be calculated and arm shape can also be determined.

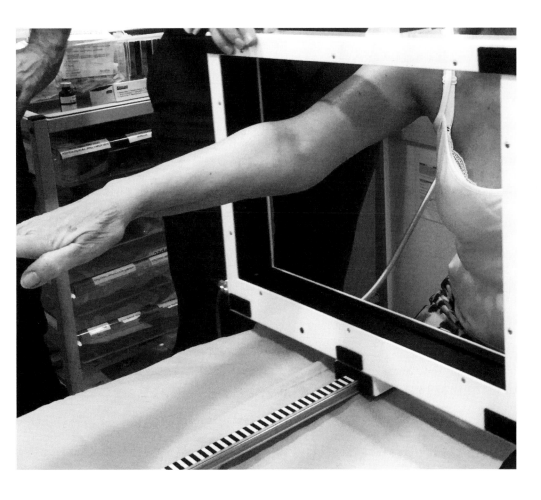

made up of multiple short-stretch fabric flaps connected to a spine, which is positioned up the back of the limb. These fabric flaps are then wrapped around the front of the limb and secured by Velcro.

One of the advantages is that it allows you to adjust the fit and pressure, which gives you much more independence with your treatment. The more firmly you close and secure the flaps, the tighter the fit and the greater the chances of seeing the swelling reduce. Furthermore because there is no elasticity involved, the wrap system does not yield and re-swelling cannot occur as it can with other garments.

COMPRESSION PUMPS

Once you have been assessed in clinic, in addition to bandages or garments, your treatment may involve using a pump. A pneumatic compression machine consists of an electrical pump connected to an inflatable sleeve (for the arm) or boot (for the leg). The sleeve or boot possesses one or more air chambers that inflate and deflate in a sequential manner controlled by the machine's software. These inflation and deflation cycles squeeze fluid out of the arm or leg.

Pump treatment requires you to be lying down or sitting, and many people choose to buy one for use at home. As such they can be a very useful aid to self-management. They do not work on their own, however; you need to have a compression garment fitted after the treatment in order to maintain any reduction in swelling.

These pumps, which are also called Intermittent Pneumatic Compression machines, have been around for

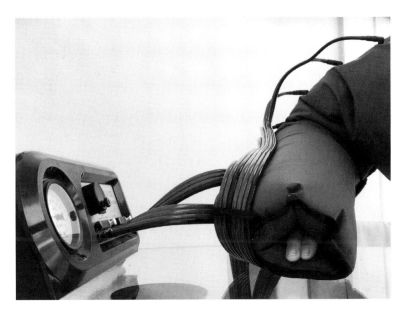

Compression pump (manufactured by Bio Compression Systems USA). The sleeve inflates at one end and the pressure then moves up the limb before deflating.

years but technology has allowed for some major advances. The result is that modern pumps work a bit like MLD but without requiring the skilled, precise movements of a therapist.

LIGHT EMITTING DIODE

Another way to stimulate your tissues is through the use of low levels of light, via a Light Emitting Diode (LED) or Low Level Laser Therapy (LLLT). Your cells absorb the light causing a biochemical reaction that changes the process of unhealthy cells and encourages healthy cells to take their place. Unlike lasers used for surgery it does not cause your tissues to heat up. Moderate evidence exists to support its effectiveness in the treatment of breast-cancer-related lymphoedema, with reductions in both swelling and pain.

KINESIOLOGY TAPING

Kinesiology Taping (KT) is an extension of a method known as Japanese Kinesiology Taping developed by chiropractor Dr Kenzo Kase, thought to help injured tissues and muscles to heal. It was originally used, and indeed still is, as a sports taping method – you will often see athletes with strips of brightly coloured tape stuck on sections of their skin.

KT involves applying a one-way stretch tape along the swollen part of the body. Rather than squeezing the skin, it is said to lift it, creating 'negative pressure' and providing more space for the fluid to move along. It sounds crazy but it works; in fact it's quite brilliant! By stretching the skin, the tape allows for improved lymph drainage when underlying muscles are used. It is particularly successful for swelling of the breast, genitals, face and hands where is it difficult to apply compression. Often people are embarrassed about their facial swelling but I remember one patient who wore bright blue tape on his face; he explained that he felt like a 'warrior' in his tape and no one was ever bold enough to ask him what it was!

ELECTRO-THERAPY

There are a number of other possible treatments that all involve some version of 'electro-therapy'. All of these treatments, such as Deep Oscillation therapy, PhysioTouch and BodyFlow, are still undergoing research but are now being used in many clinics. Like KT, they have been developed from other fields, such as sports or engineering, and adapted for lymphoedema treatments. They work in a variety of ways: some send a harmless current into the affected area to make your muscles twitch, pushing fluid along the lymph vessels; some create a vibration in the affected area to make the tissue softer; while others use suction (lifting the skin), like KT. Back in the clinic, after receiving one or more of these alternative treatments, you would be wrapped back up in a compression garment.

OTHER PRODUCTS

There are a number of new products that defy categorisation. There are devices that can measure the amount of pressure that they are exerting; that can see how warm your limb is; or tell you how much exercise you do. There are also materials that change colour according to their tension; garments that make innovative use of straps, zips, Velcro and other fastenings; and tons of other stuff. All of them could go on to change the way we treat lymphoedema in the next few years.

The good news is that lymphoedema treatment is evolving and change is happening fast – and people like me love that. It's a really exciting time to be working in this area. By increasing the number of products available, and offering more choice, we should be able to make living with lymphoedema just a little bit easier.

SURGERY

Traditionally there have been few, if any, surgical options for the treatment of lymphoedema but as Professor Dominic Furniss and Alex Ramsden of the Oxford Lymphoedema Practice explain, that is beginning to change:

It is true to say that surgery for lymphoedema is undergoing a renaissance. There is now a worldwide interest by surgeons in caring for patients with the condition.

Throughout the twentieth century, the surgical management of secondary lymphoedema was confined to salvage procedures used to treat end-stage disease. In part, this was because the operations devised for lymphoedema were highly invasive, fraught with complications, and left large scars on the affected limb. Operations essentially removed large amounts of affected tissue from limbs without any reconstruction of the lymphatic system.

The invasive nature of these operations meant that patients with mild or moderate lymphoedema did not wish to undertake surgery, and just used management techniques to control swelling. However, these therapies do not treat the underlying problem, and therefore cannot offer the possibility of cure.

A range of modern surgical techniques were developed towards the end of the twentieth century, and have been refined over the last two decades. In cases where lymphoedema is diagnosed early and there has been a limited amount of damage, these techniques offer the possibility of reconstructing the lymph system.

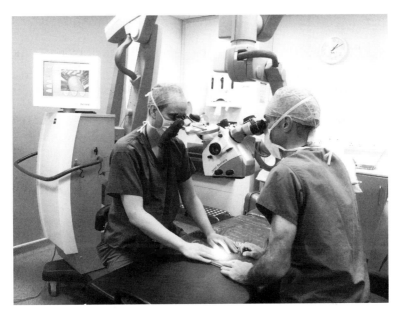

Professor Dominic Furniss (l) and Alex Ramsden (r) setting up the high-powered operating microscope prior to LVA surgery.

LYMPHATICOVENULAR ANASTOMOSIS (LVA)

LVA is a super-microsurgical technique that involves connecting lymph vessels just under the skin to small veins. This returns the lymph fluid directly to the bloodstream within the affected limb, bypassing the blocked lymph vessels. The operation can be performed under local anaesthetic through small skin incisions, and has a low risk of complications. It is technically demanding, however, and must be performed by experienced surgeons. Because lymph vessels are tiny – typically 0.5 millimetres in diameter – the entire operation is performed using the operating microscope and specialist equipment, and the sutures used to make the joins are much thinner than a human hair.

LVA has good long-term results, especially when performed in the early stages of the disease – figures suggest that over 85 per cent of patients can maintain reduced limb volumes without the use of compression garments. Also, there is high-quality evidence that in patients undergoing surgery for breast cancer, LVA can prevent the onset of lymphoedema if it is done when the lymph glands are removed.

If performed early, we think that LVA offers the opportunity to practically cure lymphoedema, as we can see in the following story, in which Emma developed lymphoedema in her thirties after treatment for breast cancer:

I developed swelling in my left arm about six months after my first surgery (mastectomy and clearance of lymph glands from my armpit). I was devastated when I developed lymphoedema and have struggled, at times, to come to terms with the diagnosis. I'm generally a positive person and flew through surgery and chemo but after dealing with a cancer diagnosis and all the treatment this seemed to be the last straw!

Having the LVA surgery has definitely been positive for me. Not only have the results of the surgery been good, but it has also given me a sense of control over my lymphoedema, instead of just being stuck with it.

I did a lot of research and met with a few surgeons before I went ahead. Overall I felt the potential risks were outweighed by the benefits. I chose the Oxford Lymphoedema Practice, as I wanted it done under local anaesthetic, plus having two surgeons increases the chances of getting more vessels connected.

In terms of the surgery I found it absolutely fine under local anaesthetic; no pain, interesting to watch the surgery and great not to feel zonked out after! The recovery is very easy. In fact I had to stop myself doing too much with my arm, as I felt completely normal after!

In terms of results, I saw a more or less immediate change in texture, from swollen and a bit hard to much softer. Also I previously had quite a bit of swelling around my elbow whereas now you can clearly see the bones again. I didn't lose much in volume but my arm wasn't that big to start with. A year on and my arm is actually smaller than the other side, and generally is more stable than previously. Plus I no longer have to wear my compression garment.

LYMPHATICO-LYMPHATIC BYPASS (LLB)

LLB is a technically demanding super-microsurgical technique, which may be suitable for early stage secondary lymphoedema. It involves taking a healthy lymph vessel from an unaffected part of the body and transplanting it to the area with lymphoedema. The healthy lymph vessel is then joined up to lymph vessels above and below the blockage. This operation requires a general anaesthetic and has a higher rate of complications, including swelling in the area from where the healthy lymph vessel was taken. Results of this operation also seem to be good and maintained in the long term, but it is not widely practised around the world.

'Towards the end of his life,
Dad found that a special massage
was a help but at that point of his illness
there was only one person in London
we could find who did this kind of
massage for lymphoedema sufferers.
He found it very beneficial and I hope
now – twenty-two years on – this is
more commonly available.'

Zoe Wanamaker

LYMPH NODE TRANSFER (LNT)

This operation involves taking healthy lymph glands from one part of the body and transplanting them to the area affected by lymphoedema. No surgical connections are made between the imported lymph glands and the remaining lymph vessels. Instead it is thought that the transplanted glands somehow stimulate new lymph vessels to form. Once grown, these new lymph vessels connect to lymph vessels that previously had their drainage channels blocked.

This operation requires somewhat less technical expertise than either LVA or LLB, so it has been more widely adopted throughout the world. LNT is performed under general anaesthetic, and requires several days in hospital. It has some significant complications, including the possible development of lymphoedema in the limb from where the lymph glands were taken.

The results of this operation are reasonable when performed soon after lymphoedema has developed, but we think that this technique has little to recommend it above LVA or LLB.

LIPOSUCTION

Liposuction is an alternative surgical option used in later stage lymphoedema, when the lymph vessels are no longer functioning very well, and therefore reconstructive techniques will not be effective. Also, by this stage, fat has often become the dominant component of the swelling.

The technique involves making several small incisions in the affected limb, under general anaesthetic. Small tubes are inserted through the incisions under the skin to suck out the fat. The patient is immediately placed in compression bandages, and then compression garments are fitted.

Liposuction can reduce the size of the limb completely down to normal. It only removes the solid element – because the lymph vessels remain damaged, fluid is still present – but without the fat the remaining fluid is easier to control by compression. So with this surgery, compression garments will still have to be worn to control the swelling.

Liposuction is a reliable, proven technique that gives predictable results when used for highly selected patients (i.e. those whose swelling is predominantly composed of fat rather than fluid).

FUTURE DEVELOPMENTS

To maximise their chances of recovery, patients need surgical care as soon as possible, so the early detection of the condition in those at high risk is key (see page 60). Achieving this will require the implementation of a comprehensive screening programme, as well as educating at-risk patients and the professionals who care for them. Advances in imaging will improve our ability to detect and accurately locate functioning lymph vessels, making reconstructive lymphatic surgery more accurate and predictable. Technical advances in equipment used in this surgery should allow smaller vessels to be connected with greater accuracy, improving outcomes in lymphoedema surgery.

As you can see, although there isn't a cure, there are a number of new ways to tackle lymphoedema that will hopefully become more mainstream, and continue to develop into ever more effective treatments. However, in the meantime there is one more thing that has been shown to really help, which sufferers can do themselves: in obese patients, the single most effective treatment can be to lose weight.

9

Managing Obesity and Lymphoedema

As we've seen, obesity and lymphoedema are very much interrelated – not only can obesity cause lymphoedema, but lymphoedema can also increase weight gain, in a vicious circle. Swelling is also harder to treat in obese patients as they find it harder to exercise, and compression garments are harder to fit on larger limbs. However, weight loss can have a very beneficial effect for these patients, so combining a manageable exercise regime with a nutritious diet is key.

WEIGHT LOSS

Professor James Levine MD PhD, director of Obesity Solutions at the Mayo Clinic and Arizona State University, shares the story of one of his patients whose life was transformed by a manageable weight loss intervention, along with some of the lessons we can learn:

I was early in my career, working in a hospital in London, when I met a patient called Maureen who came into the Weight Management Clinic. Maureen was originally from Glasgow and had relocated to London when her husband took a job there. Maureen, now in her fifties, had battled with severe obesity for thirty years. She was more than 75 kg above her ideal weight. She entered my surgery in a wheelchair, unable to walk. Maureen had attempted to lose weight thirty-four times, each time using a different approach. On the few occasions that she had lost weight, she soon regained it all, often ending up even heavier. Maureen was essentially housebound. She had wanted to become more active but her swollen legs had stopped her. She felt that she just couldn't win, and now was desperate for help.

Two nursing aides helped Maureen onto the examination table; she told me that most doctors wouldn't examine or even touch her. Although she had significant obesity in her abdomen it seemed most of her excess body weight was from the hips down – she was barely able to move her legs. When I examined her, the leg fat had a softer, more pliable texture than normally occurs with obesity. It didn't quite add up.

We took a specialised type of X-ray scan, which accurately measures leg fat and leg fluid, and we discovered a combination of excess fat and fluid; while Maureen did have significant excess body fat in her legs she also had massive lymphoedema. I explained to her how obesity and lymphoedema are interrelated and her next question was inevitable: 'Can you help me?'

In normal cases of obesity, a weight-loss plan is immediately put in place. However, in this instance, Maureen was urgently referred to our lymphoedema specialists first. They got to work with massage therapy, a special pumping apparatus and bandaging of the lower extremities. Two weeks later the patient returned to see me. From lymphoedema treatment alone, Maureen had already lost 10 kg.

The change was dramatic; for the first time in four months she could walk.

Now that she was mobile, and her lymphoedema treatment was underway, the Weight Management Team began to help Maureen develop a personalised weight-loss plan. The first step was for her to meet a behavioural therapist who spoke with Maureen about her tendency to eat when she was either sad or bored. The therapist encouraged and arranged for her to join a behavioural modification group to help her learn how she could adapt her behaviours to help her health. For example, now when Maureen was bored she got out her knitting needles rather than a snack.

Maureen next met with our dietician and started to log all of her foods for a week. The dietician then made some specific nutritional recommendations: for instance, Maureen tended to drink fizzy drinks and after some coaxing she switched to water as her primary drink. However, her greatest love in life (after her family) was chocolate – 650 kcal every day! The dietician and behavioural therapist help her satisfy her craving with a stick of Kit-Kat after each meal (50 kcal/stick), although part of the trick is to encourage people to stop buying chocolates and biscuits in the first place.

I also noticed that Maureen took six different types of vitamins and supplements which cost her £16 per week. I recommended she stop all of these; they were expensive, they did not help her health and in fact some supplements can actually interfere with prescribed medicines.

However, what made the greatest change to Maureen's life was sending her to the physical therapy team. They worked with her on a programme of gentle strength train-ing, conditioning and mobility. Maureen, like most of my patients, could not afford to go to a gym or a swimming pool. Even if it was free, she told me she wouldn't go to the gym because, 'People look at me bad.' After helping her stretch, the physical therapy team gave Maureen an achievable activity goal. Taking into account the fact that she had been unable to walk for four months, her initial programme was simply five minutes of gentle stretching three times per day and two-minute walks six times per day. Maureen took her walks strolling around her living room before and after breakfast, lunch and dinner. This programme may seem trivial, but for someone who hasn't walked in months, patients have to start with achievable goals. We had to teach Maureen how to win her life back.

Over the first four weeks, a catalogue of changes occurred in Maureen. She kept going to the lymphoedema specialist, where the massage, pumping and bandaging continued. Significant weight loss, 15 kg, was attributed to the lymphoedema treatment alone. Maureen started cooking again. She walked down to the supermarket (a ten-minute walk) twice a week when the weather was OK and bought fresh fruit and veg – but no chocolate! Being able to walk was critical for her. Before coming to our clinic, Maureen had no mobility or energy and so home-delivered food like pizza was her only option. Now that she had energy and 'zip', she cooked healthy food, and taking on healthful behaviours started to come naturally.

Over the next four months Maureen went from strength to strength; her micro-walks across the living room became six 10-minute walks each day. Every day, when the weather permitted, she walked outside, most often to the high street to get the paper or go to the supermarket. If it rained outside, she would potter around the flat folding laundry or doing similar activities. She revived her social life too. One night while browsing on-line, she found a group of knitters who met twice a week at a nearby coffee shop. Maureen joined the group and walked to the meetings. Maureen was getting her legs back and her confidence with it. Oh, and did I mention she had lost 30 kg? As she put it: 'The weight just melted off.'

Maureen entered my surgery for her six-month visit, a new person. She strode in, beaming. She had not been able to work for two years but now she was a volunteer nurse assistant at her local hospital. She'd also been able to take up an old hobby of hers, going to junk shops in search of treasures, which she hadn't done in years.

Throughout her treatment, we had given Maureen a gadget to measure her daily activity levels. Before her treatment began, with debilitating lymphoedema and uncontrolled obesity, Maureen essentially sat all day long. Six months later and 30 kg lighter, she had halved her sitting time. Without realising it, she was walking for one-to-two hours every day, without breaking a sweat or spending a pound. More importantly, she had massively increased the amount of fun in her life.

After one year of lymphoedema and obesity treatment, Maureen had lost a total of 45 kg and was working part time. Her new healthier behaviours had had an effect on her husband Robert as well, who had also lost weight.

Maureen mailed me a picture of her wearing a huge sunhat in Florida. She was in the playground with her two-year-old grandson. On the back of the postcard she wrote, 'This is living.'

Maureen's case illustrates ten key issues relevant to obesity and lymphoedema:

1. Obesity and lymphoedema are directly linked. Obesity can make lymphoedema worse and lymphoedema can make body fat grow.
2. People can have obesity and lymphoedema and not have cancer.
3. People who undergo surgery or who have been treated for cancer are far more likely to develop lymphoedema if they have obesity.
4. In a patient with lymphoedema and obesity, the lymphoedema must be treated.
5. In a patient with obesity, weight loss helps improve lymphoedema regardless of the cause.
6. Improving physical activity is critical for helping a patient with obesity and lymphoedema. This is true even without weight loss.
7. With respect to improving nutrition, there are no magic solutions. There are no special vitamin preparations or supplements.
8. In the same way that everyone is different in how they eat, people differ in how best to adjust what they eat. Behavioural specialists and dieticians can really help find a sustainable approach to suit individual needs.

9. The best way to improve physical activity is to find something active that you like to do and that can be easily incorporated into your daily routine. Start slowly (sometimes very, very slowly) and gradually build up.

10. Weight and lymphoedema do not accumulate overnight and will not vanish overnight either. Weight loss is a bit like a savings account, the more you invest over time, the more benefit you reap in the long term. Build your new life one brick at a time!

Many years after I originally met Maureen, I was standing in line for coffee in a shopping centre when someone tapped me on the shoulder. I turned round and at first didn't recognise the woman grinning at me. She looked fantastic and, more importantly, happy. Maureen wasn't slim by magazine standards; she had healthy curves. She was happy, healthy, attractive and having a great time.

As we have seen, obesity is a real problem when it comes to lymphoedema, and weight loss is an important first step in alleviating some of these problems. But lymphoedema sufferers don't just have to contend with physical challenges like these. Living with the condition can also have a huge psychological impact.

10

Living with Lymphoedema

Although there are treatments for lymphoedema, living with the condition still presents a whole range of daily challenges for patients, both physical and psychological. Some of these may seem trivial to an outsider at first but when even the act of finding a new pair of shoes seems like an impossible task, the condition starts to take its toll. In fact it can be hard for some sufferers to find any kind of clothing to fit over their swelling, while others are reluctant to wear anything that will make their swelling very visible – a particular problem in hot weather.

There are many other day-to-day problems that vary according to the site and severity of the swelling and the age and overall fitness of the patient. An elderly patient, for example, might find that the extra weight of a swollen limb affects their balance, making them more likely to suffer falls.

A swollen hand, meanwhile, can affect your grip, making it difficult to do even the simplest things such as open a jar, write a shopping list, get washed or put on clothes.

Some people find that their lymphoedema makes it impossible to work, and may even make it necessary to retire on medical grounds. If you are a healthcare professional, for example, you might need to work bare to the elbows but this is not possible if you have to wear a compression sleeve.

Travelling – especially air travel – can also be difficult given that sitting still can exacerbate your swelling. This means that many sufferers are reluctant to risk long journeys, or are forced to accept the discomfort and then undertake a day or two of exercise to get their swelling back under control. Holidays can also be a challenge – most of us prefer a warm getaway, but the increased heat can be a real problem for lymphoedema sufferers, as it can increase the swelling. Insect bites also tend to be more common in such climates, and these can be extremely painful if you have lymphoedema, leading to a considerable increase in your swelling and raising your risk of a bout of cellulitis.

These physical problems are bad enough, but the psychological impact can be just as debilitating. As Professor Stebbing, an oncologist at Imperial College London, notes, 'Lymphoedema requires lifelong care and psychosocial support. In addition to swelling and increased risk of infection, physical consequences include a sensation of heaviness, pain, discomfort, restricted mobility, and loss of function. But there are also serious psychosocial consequences, including psychological distress, social embarrassment, poor body image, social isolation and financial burden.'

One thing that can be helpful is to have people willing to speak out about their experiences, so that sufferers feel there is someone who knows what they're going through, someone they can relate to.

A CHAMPION FOR LYMPHOEDEMA

It is not often that celebrities admit that they have lymphoedema but not every celebrity is like Kathy Bates, Oscar-winning actress and advocate for lymphoedema. Here is her story:

I have lymphoedema. I developed it right after a bilateral mastectomy in 2012. I knew what lymphoedema was because my mother underwent a radical mastectomy in the seventies. The surgeon had scraped all the tissue from the left side of her body from the armpit to the middle of her chest down to the bone. The scarring was terrible. My mother's arm swelled to twice its size. With no treatment in those days, I watched as her spirit diminished with the realisation that she would have to live with this for the rest of her life. She may have felt like I did, that her life was over. It may seem trivial to some, but the worst thing to her was she'd never be able to wear 'smart' clothes again because her arm wouldn't fit in the sleeve. By that time I had already left home and was involved with my career. I will always regret not fully understanding what she was going through, not being with her to take care of her. Knowing what I know now there are so many things I could have done to help her.

When I was diagnosed with ovarian cancer in 2003, I was in a difficult relationship with a man who had survived melanoma, but suffered severe lymphoedema in his left arm. He lived on pain medication. He was stubborn and worn out with seeing doctors, so he tried to manage it himself with bandages. His arm was in terrible shape. Heavy as wood, it pulled his shoulder down almost out of joint. His skin was extremely sensitive to the touch and sometimes oozed lymph. After some years the relationship ended, but it took me a long time to recover from the trauma.

When I was diagnosed with breast cancer, the malignancy just happened to be in my left breast. What a horrifying irony it would be to look down at a swollen arm just like his and for the rest of my life be reminded of a time I so wanted to forget.

I remember telling my surgeon on three separate occasions exactly why I didn't want him to take any more lymph nodes than necessary. I overshared to make my case. I pleaded with him, 'If the sentinel node is clear, get out.'

In those first couple of days while I was recovering in the hospital, I would suddenly feel a throbbing knot of pain in the back of my hand for a few seconds and then it would pass. Then another knot would throb in the shaft of my thumb and go out like a light. These twinkling lights of pain ran up and down my arms for the first day or two. I was terribly worried.

During my first check-up, my surgeon told me unfortunately he felt it necessary to remove nineteen lymph nodes from my left armpit and three from my right. I went ballistic. Screaming at him. Wailing. Devastated. Trying to get off the table pushing at everybody. I heard him shout, 'I cured you of cancer! I cured you of cancer!'

More people came in the room to hold me down and quiet me. Over my shoulder I heard a ridiculous little voice saying, 'Just breathe.' I turned and saw a social worker who clearly had nothing to offer but that, and no comprehension of what I was going through. I thought, none of you do! No one in that room. Not my best friend of some thirty years. Not my niece. Not the doctors. Even though I had told them and told them. Not one of them had understood what this meant to me. How devastating this news was. They had all betrayed me. Was this how my mother had felt?

Kathy Bates, wearing a compression sleeve.

I shoved them all out of my way and ran to the elevator. Down on the street I began to walk. Anywhere. I was enraged. Abandoned. I didn't know where to go. It was the middle of summer. Boiling hot. I was feeling weak and in excruciating pain. I still had the 'grenades' in to drain the fluid from the incisions. I realised I would have to go home or else back to surgery if I ripped any stitches. I don't remember what happened after that. How they got me in the car. How I got home.

Looking back on that day as I write this, I understand my violent reaction was locked and loaded by the post-traumatic stress of my abusive relationship. I was blind to everything and everyone else. My surgeon's job and his sole focus were on curing me of cancer. I want to make it absolutely clear that sharing my reaction here does not in any way mean I blame him for developing lymphoedema. For him, curing me of cancer was the goal. Making sure that I survived. Everything else was secondary. God knows I will always be grateful to him for that. Because of him I am here to tell you my story.

I've learned that the lymphatic system, unlike the blood system, is an open system, but among the many vital functions it provides there is also a downside. It is a highway for cancer cells to travel to other organs where they metastasise. That is why my surgeon, like many, erred on the side of caution.

My recovery was difficult. With my breasts gone and now lymphoedema, I felt trapped in a body I wanted to escape. One of my doctors found Dr Emily Iker, who is a cancer survivor and lymphoedema patient as well as a committed and dedicated doctor. I was still pretty shut down and angry when I first met her. She listened to me vent my anger while I told her my story about why this was especially awful for me.

Then she said in her charming Czech accent, 'My dear that is all in the past. You are here now. Have a glass of champagne and begin your new life.' That brought me up short. I looked at her. It was probably the first time I had really looked at anyone since that horrible day. Her face was full of light and humour. No time to waste. A delightful let's-get-to-it attitude.

I began manual lymph drainage followed by a sleeve pump twice a week at the beginning to get the swelling under control; then less and less often until I got to the point of maintenance. Four years later, I still suffer from lymphoedema, but thanks to catching it early my arms aren't terribly swollen. I had a bout of cellulitis a few years ago, but antibiotics cleared it up. I have to wear compression sleeves when my arms swell due to heat or stress from overuse or lifting things I shouldn't. Of course I wear them while flying. They are hard to put on by myself, but I've gotten better at it.

Dr Iker introduced me to Bill Repicci and LE&RN (see page 47). He asked me to become their spokesperson. Bill told me that upwards of 10 million Americans suffer with lymphoedema – more than muscular dystrophy, multiple sclerosis, ALS, Parkinson's and AIDS combined. An estimated 140 million worldwide. I was gobsmacked.

Bill explained that most general practitioners are uneducated about lymphoedema. In four years of medical school, young doctors spend between fifteen minutes to half an hour on the lymphatic system, so it is not included on most state licensing exams. This means if you have a swollen limb or swelling in your groin or neck and go to your doctor, often he or she won't be able to help you or might suggest you go home and put hot compresses on it. They might tell you to lose some weight. Time goes by.

The swelling gets worse. Now you have to find another doctor who might know how to help you. This can go on untreated for years, as your lymphoedema gets worse. I am still astounded at how often this happens. How millions suffer needlessly. You would think it should be simple to get all the GPs together and let them know what to look out for. Easier said than done. As diseases go, lymphoedema is at the bottom of the list.

Some doctors know what lymphoedema is, but they believe it is merely a cosmetic issue and rarely fatal. I'd like to say to them, 'Would you like to be one of those few rare cases who die of sepsis?' For the rest of us lucky ones it is a life sentence. Lymphoedema affects our quality of life every day, day after day. It is debilitating and disfiguring. Sometimes we win the day with optimism. Some days it defeats us. The psychological effects of having one's life interrupted by this disease and not being taken seriously by the very doctors we expect to help us, drains us of the energy we need to help ourselves.

Through LE&RN I have found amazing individuals in the lymphoedema community who suffer, but who manage to find a way to bypass the limits their disease puts on their plans for life. There are two memorable individuals whose words will stay with me forever.

Pearl-Ann Hinds is a young dancer who developed lymphoedema in one leg. After months of being too embarrassed to dance, she decided to choreograph and perform a modern dance on YouTube called 'Hello World'. She says, 'If I continued to hide the reality, the power to change the legs of future generations would be lost.'

Emma Detlefsen is a child who was born with lymphoedema in both legs. She often battles infections that cause her to be hospitalised. But she has become a powerful advocate for LE&RN. She says, 'If I can do something hard like walk back and forth across the Brooklyn Bridge maybe a smart scientist can do something hard for them and find a cure for this disease in my lifetime.'

We are struggling to raise the research dollars to find a cure for lymphoedema, but there is a ray of hope. While making a speech at the National Institutes of Health, I learned that researchers may one day have the opportunity to discover the pivotal role of the lymphatic system in the treatment of cancer metastasis, AIDS, auto-immune diseases, obesity, cardiovascular disease, organ transplants as well as those of us suffering from cancer-related lymphoedema or congenital lymphoedema. Researchers' discoveries may unlock a Pandora's box of cures for a host of diseases. These pathological heavy-hitters might finally draw attention to our plight, the plight of millions. I look forward to that day.

A THERAPIST'S APPROACH

It's important that doctors and specialists acknowledge the wide-ranging psychological impact of lymphoedema. Carmel Phelan, a lymphoedema therapist, explains how the right approach and attitude can help a patient to deal with the condition:

A lymphoedema practitioner is expected to wear many hats. Qualities such as empathy and compassion and having an innovative approach are essential. The ability to put yourself in that person's shoes, to make a positive connection at that initial assessment is so important.

It is vital that I, as a therapist, understand that some people have already been through an emotionally and physically traumatic, and sometimes life-threatening, situation. To come through cancer treatment, for example, which may involve surgery, chemotherapy, radiotherapy, or all three, and then to be faced with lymphoedema, is a very difficult challenge – one that many find very distressing and harder to deal with than their cancer treatment.

I am shocked to find that some people still come to the initial session expecting that MLD will involve a syringe and pump to withdraw the fluid as a one-off treatment that will permanently fix the condition. Fluid cannot be drained off for the same reason that fluid cannot be drained from a jelly (which is 99 per cent water) without melting it. Lymphoedema fluid does not lie free in lakes within the swelling but is integrated within the tissues.

When a person sees the compression sleeve for the first time they often say, 'You really don't expect me to wear that do you? There must be a better and quicker way of fixing this condition.'

The realisation that there is no cure (at present) and they have lymphoedema for life, is a daunting prospect for all patients. Some are distraught and often break down in tears. There is no doubt that the psychological effect of the diagnosis can have a hugely negative impact, especially when it comes to body image. A breast removed can be concealed or substituted, but a swollen arm or hand cannot be hidden. Coming to terms with this situation is difficult enough without the added problem of being unable to find clothes to fit. All this added stress undermines their recovery from a long cancer treatment journey.

I see the role of the lymphoedema practitioner as an equal holistic partnership with the patient. Compassion and an understanding of the challenges a person with lymphoedema faces are key to successful management, while empowering the individual to self-manage their condition to the best of their ability.

Lymphoedema is a life-long condition so it is necessary for patients to make changes and adjustments to their lifestyle, but these don't have to be huge; they need to be realistic and sustainable. The condition can be managed if you can find what works best for you and incorporate that into your daily life. For most people this will be the regular wearing of a compression garment and avoiding circumstances that exacerbate swelling, for example, getting run down or overtired, long-haul air travel, insect bites, exercising without a compression sleeve, or sunburn, to name a few.

Even if you have been successfully managing your condition for years, it is important not to become complacent. You need to remember that you are still at risk of exacerbating your lymphoedema if you damage your arm or suffer infection. On the other hand it is important that you are able to lead as normal a life as possible and not let the lymphoedema beat you!

The greatest reward for me as a lymphoedema practitioner is when I have successfully assisted a person to find the key to self-managing their condition with little on-going help from me.

FINDING A VOICE

One problem that lymphoedema sufferers sometimes face is the feeling that they have to deal with the condition alone – perhaps it is embarrassment about their condition, perhaps they have don't have access to any information about it, or, in the case of cancer survivors, perhaps they just don't want to be judged for complaining.

Cancer treatment is a long and uncomfortable journey and those who develop lymphoedema are left with a constant reminder of that time. But, more importantly, it also gives them yet another challenge to face, and one that they are often expected to accept as the price of curing their cancer. In reality, lymphoedema remains one of the major distressing side effects of cancer treatment.

Psychodynamic Counsellor Sue Wilkinson is well aware of the damaging effects of bottling up negative emotions, and how important it is not to become isolated when facing a difficult change in your life.

Lymphoedema is a condition that is too often not talked about in the open – almost as if the compression garment people wear is tightly compressing their feelings as well. They don't feel able to reveal how it's really affecting them.

I wonder if this may link to a sense of survivor's guilt, that having beaten cancer they should feel lucky, grateful even, acknowledging those who did not make it. Therefore they should not complain about this non-fatal condition.

This is a sentiment that often seems to be reinforced by practitioners in the world of medicine and other observers.

But is it healthy to expect sufferers to hide away their completely natural reactions of anger, resentment, anxiety and fear? They are not getting a chance to properly process their feelings.

There must be moments when the sun shines, and they long to bare their arms, but don't want to make their compression sleeve public. They might long to buy that new dress or shirt, knowing that they can't fit their swollen limb inside. They might scold themselves, repressing these feelings and desires as trivial, narcissistic or ungrateful.

Lymphoedema is not a killer. It can be dismissed as unimportant, especially compared to 'more serious' diseases like cancer. People might worry that they'll be judged for complaining, seen as ungrateful, or a bother; they think that this is something that must be endured stoically and in silence, displaying the traditional British stiff upper lip.

But the danger of this attitude is that it's very isolating. It can leave sufferers to handle their feelings alone.

We all have lines of defence to protect ourselves, both physically and emotionally. People hide their true emotions, afraid of what other people's reactions might be. But this can stop us from letting others in, from helping us to cope in difficult times.

For sufferers of lymphoedema whose body has betrayed them, there can be a lack of trust in themselves and others. Even those in a long-term relationship might find it hard to share their feelings with their partner, or to engage

'Seven years ago my wife, Kate, developed breast cancer which affected her lymph glands and required surgery. We knew very little about lymphoedema; a book like this would have been enormous help to us and I have no doubt whatsoever that it will be to many others.'

Baron Charles Guthrie

in the intimacy of a sexual relationship, perhaps worried whether their partner still desires them and can cope with the changes to their once-familiar bodies.

The changes, both physical and psychological, that lymphoedema sufferers must endure will be hard to come to terms with, and may also be hard for their partners to understand. Are you still the same person you were before? 'You have changed' can hold a ring of attack, but there is some truth in this. They are changed; this condition has had a big impact on them.

There is no going back. The way to move forward is to find a way to trust others, to open up, to process all the feelings and emotions that lymphoedema has thrown into turmoil. Patients need to see that they don't have to suffer alone. They don't need to accept their condition as collateral damage, the price they must pay in return for surviving cancer.

Hopefully this book will encourage people to let their voice be heard. A talking cure of sorts, emboldening them to let others help them, to express their negative emotions without fear of judgement.

MAINTAINING INTIMATE RELATIONSHIPS

There are so many aspects of lymphoedema that patients can struggle to deal with. One of those is learning to come to terms with the changes in their bodies and feeling comfortable in maintaining an intimate relationship. This is a very important step, as Catherine Hood from the London Oncology Centre (LOC) explains:

How good is your sex life? This is a surprisingly difficult question to answer. People often worry about comparisons, whether they will meet the expectations of others let alone the expectations for themselves. However, each couple's sex life is unique; what works for one pair may not for another. If there is one thing I've learned in many years of working with individuals and couples with sexual problems it is that there is no 'normal'. Every sex life is individual, important and deeply personal.

It's difficult to escape the fear of judgement when discussing sex. Perhaps this fear, coupled with the natural embarrassment of talking about something so personal, is why few patients brave a conversation with their doctors about sexual issues. Arguably more pertinent is the fear of causing offence and the worry about not being able to answer a person's questions that stops doctors from routinely encouraging a discussion about intimacy with their patients. However, a person's intimate life is important and it is all too often affected by long-term conditions such as lymphoedema.

It's no surprise that a strong link has been demonstrated between a person's body image and their sexual confidence and willingness to engage in sexual activity. The better you feel about yourself the more confident you are going to be at letting go emotionally and physically with a partner, something that is important to the enjoyment of true intimacy. If a person doesn't feel confident about their body then their libido may suffer. This is often particularly true of women. If a woman is distracted by feelings of being unattractive or unsexy then she is going to find it harder to relax and engage in sexual thought and arousal.

Lymphoedema can affect the way a person feels about their body. It takes time to adjust to how the body looks and wearing compression garments may make it harder to feel sexy.

Those in a relationship might worry about the impact of lymphoedema on their intimate lives, while those not in a relationship may worry about how they will be attractive to a new partner and how to bring up the subject.

It's worth saying that a couple's sex life isn't a static entity. It changes throughout life and has to adapt to life challenges such as childbirth, ageing, ill health and disability. Communication is essential for couples and individuals to adjust – to acknowledge and accept what has changed and to then be able to see and explore the new opportunities in the future. A person's sexual life can be challenged by physical changes such as lymphoedema but adaptations can bring new delights. As they learn to manage better physically then their sex life should improve too.

Below are a few tips that may ease the journey and help retain or restore a satisfying intimate life:

1. Talk about sex early. Doctors and healthcare professionals need to be able to open a discussion about sex with their patients, and individuals should feel encouraged to ask questions in return. Maintaining an uncomfortable silence about sexual side-effects might make it harder for those with conditions such as lymphoedema to ask questions and seek answers and support. Often simple advice can make a big difference.

   If you feel uncomfortable discussing these private issues with your doctor then seek the help of a sexual counsellor, psychosexual practitioner or therapist; there may be somebody trained in discussing sexual problems at your clinic so be brave and ask.

2. Discuss your fears and concerns with your partner. Partners often worry about how to show their affection while the other is distressed. Allowing both parties to discuss their feelings can reduce anxiety, maintain emotional intimacy and allow both to adapt to the new situation following treatment. This may be difficult and again, the help of a counsellor, psychosexual practitioner or therapist may help.

3. Stay intimate. Kissing and cuddling is a way to show your affection even if you don't feel like having intercourse. Non-sexual massage can also be a way to

help you feel close to each other. Massage can also allow both of you to safely learn what feels pleasurable and what areas of the body are uncomfortable.

4.   Make time for intimacy. Plan times when the lymphoedema is at its best. Some find their swelling is better first thing in the morning or have sex after wearing a compression garment for a while. Make the most of the times when you feel at your best.

5.   Boost your sexual confidence. Prepare for intimacy in ways that make you feel body confident. It may be luxuriating in a shower or bath or wearing some alluring underwear to cover areas of your body you feel less confident about while boosting your feelings of attractiveness.

6.   Adjust your sexual positions to maximise comfort. It may be uncomfortable to put pressure on areas of lymphoedema. Learning about each other's bodies will help you experiment and explore new methods of arousal and pleasurable positions for intercourse.

7.   Use plenty of lubrication. If sex is dry or uncomfortable use good-quality, natural water-based lubricants and vaginal moisturisers.

8.   Restore the balance. Plan dates and events with your partner that don't involve hospitals, doctors or treatments. Take the time to reconnect and see each other as a couple again. The body may have changed but the essence of who you are as a couple hasn't.

9.   Seek help and support. If sex still proves a challenge, or you or your partner are struggling to adjust and adapt, then talking about your problems and

receiving specialist advice can help. Sexual problems are well recognised and there are many counsellors and healthcare professionals trained in psychosexual issues who can help.

Associate Professor Kerry Sherman, a health psychologist from Macquarie University, Sydney, Australia regularly encounters people experiencing these problems:

Sufferers of lymphoedema have many physical problems to deal with, and sometimes they worry that being upset about their body image and changes can seem trivial in comparison. But it's so important to accept these changes and love your body just as it is. Once you can do that, it's easier to believe that others can also love you and accept you just as you are. These are the sorts of issues I work through with my patients. Take for example Wendy, who was diagnosed with breast cancer three years ago and developed lymphoedema in her right arm within a year.

My name is Wendy, I'm thirty-four years old and lymphoedema is my constant companion, an uninvited guest wherever I go. My lymphoedema affects my life in different ways, but right now I would like to tell you about the intimate side of my life.

Just to paint the picture, most of the time my lymphoedema is well managed, partly due to my constant wearing of a compression garment. It's not the most attractive thing to wear and I'm very conscious that it's like a beacon telling the world that something is wrong with my arm. When I'm wearing the garment it's hard not to think about lymphoedema and breast cancer, but I actively try not to dwell on this. I do feel a bit of a frump though when I'm wearing the garment and it seems to me that it has about zero sex appeal.

Needless to say, I'm not a huge fan of what I see of my body when I look in the mirror these days; I really don't see myself as being sexy any more. It's a bit of a problem as I find it a struggle to think of myself as being a 'turn on' for my husband. Lucky for me, he thinks otherwise. Somehow he manages to see right past my lumpy arm and thinks of me as the same sexy, beautiful woman that he married eight years ago. He has been so understanding and helpful, and little by little I'm getting my mojo back, so to speak.

Sometimes we just have lots of hugs and we don't have intercourse. He senses that sometimes it's just all too difficult for me, but those hugs are very special for us, and have really helped to keep our intimacy alive and well. One day when the kids were away with the grandparents we decided to have a swim in our pool and I got brave and put on my bikini. I felt a bit scared and very self-conscious putting it on, but my husband loved it and kept telling me how gorgeous I looked. So I keep saying to myself, 'you're good, you're good', it's just lymphoedema.

A friend of mine had gynaecological cancer and has developed lymphoedema in her leg as a result of the surgery and treatment for the cancer. She has had similar experiences to me, feeling distinctly unattractive and struggling with feeling sexy. Something that has helped her a lot is joining a Facebook group for people with lymphoedema. It has really helped her to feel connected with other people who understand and have similar experiences.

Some women with lymphoedema put sex in the 'too hard' basket, but they have come to accept this, and so have their partners. Other women have found ways around the difficulties of having a swollen leg, with one friend even joking with her husband about whether it is a compression garment on, or off night (a cue for wanting sex!). Getting your partner to help with the lymphatic massage can also be very sensual and has helped a lot of couples deal with the changes to the woman's body after lymphoedema and cancer.

So in all honesty, lymphoedema doesn't have to mean the end of your sex life. It just takes care, kindness and understanding, and lots of communication between the couple. And a bit of laughter here and there never goes astray.

Lymphoedema can have a serious impact on so many aspects of a patient's life, both physical and emotional. Nowhere is that more clear than when it comes to children suffering from the condition.

11

Children with Lymphoedema

L ymphoedema in children is rare but when it does occur, the needs of the child and parents are often quite different from adults. The cause of lymphoedema in children is usually genetic, resulting in a failure of the lymph system to form properly. The good news is that in some cases, as the child grows and the lymph system matures and gets stronger, the body can learn to cope, which means that for some children, their fluid problems will disappear. Others, however, will have to deal with the condition for life.

DIFFICULTIES BEFORE BIRTH

Sometimes abnormalities of the lymph system exist even before birth and can be detected in an ultrasound. Most commonly it will just affect a small area, such as a swollen foot, but sometimes there may be extensive weakness in the lymph system throughout the body, in which case the internal organs, such as the heart, lungs or digestive tract, will also contain too much fluid. If this happens, the child may be very sick and require a lot of care. This condition is known as hydrops fetalis or universal oedema of the newborn and it can lead to a miscarriage or cause immediate and serious health issues for the baby if it is carried to term:

A problem was identified before Arabella's birth when an ultrasound examination identified hydrops. Her parents, both doctors, knew immediately that this was a life-threatening situation as they had lost two previous babies to the same condition.

However, this time they knew someone who could help them. While still in the womb, Arabella had groundbreaking surgery, performed by Professor Kypros Nicolaides, to release the fluid compressing her heart and lungs. This operation was crucial to her survival.

Arabella was born swollen all over like a Michelin tyre. She still had fluid around her lungs, in her tummy and under the skin, affecting all four limbs, face and body. She was very sick in the early stages, mainly due to difficulties in breathing caused by inadequate lymph drainage from the lungs. She also had a lymph problem affecting her internal organs, which caused difficulties in the way she digested and absorbed nutrients from her food, leading to diarrhoea and low protein levels in the blood.

Against all the odds Arabella survived but continued to suffer breathing difficulties and the size of her swollen limbs made movement difficult.

GROWING UP WITH LYMPHOEDEMA

Children growing up with lymphoedema can struggle during key developmental stages; as much of a struggle as it is for adults learning to cope with a swollen limb, it can be even harder for children learning to grasp basic life skills with this obstacle in their path, particularly when it affects significant parts of the body.

Lymphoedema of the hands, for example, brings its own specific problems as illustrated by Rafael's story, told by his mother:

Rafael was a big baby at birth weighing 4 kg. At three months he started suffering from terrible eczema and then, at about six months old, one of his thighs swelled to about twice the size of the other one. His hands and arms were also very chubby. Despite seeing at least three paediatricians, for different reasons, none of them suspected lymphoedema. At nine months old I knew there was something very wrong because his hands were like footballs. A fourth paediatrician finally diagnosed primary lymphoedema.

I was very worried at that time and couldn't believe there was nothing that could be done, and so organised his first lymphatic massage at the hospital in Prague, where I am from. We went every day for three weeks and he also had his hands and arms bandaged. I learned bandaging so well that I was sometimes better than the therapists, who didn't know what pressure to use and Rafael would be in pain or get blisters.

Rafael couldn't crawl until he was thirteen months old because of the imbalance in his body and the weight of his arms and leg. He weighed 15 kg at this stage because of the fluid. The lymphoedema in his arms, hands, right thigh and bottom caused such weakness and imbalance that he was only able to sit. I decided to take him back to Prague and started visiting a Vojta physiotherapy specialist, which is an essential exercise for children with cerebral palsy. He started crawling in three weeks and walking in two months. I exercised with him five times a day. From the age of two I signed him up for gymnastics, which helped him so much with balance as well as muscle strengthening and coordination, especially in his arms. He has been taking swimming lessons and now can even play tennis, despite his swollen hands.

Hand and arm lymphoedema is psychologically very difficult for children because they look different. You can see the swelling very clearly. Many people are not aware of the condition and just stare, trying to work out what's wrong. My son is very aware that he looks different and in weak moments says how ugly and fat he looks, which makes me utterly sad. I think that psychological help should be part of the care for paediatric lymphoedema patients.

Despite these problems Rafael has always been a very chatty, happy and social child, which has helped us to survive the many hospital visits and doctors. He is extremely intelligent and makes us very happy with his school results and talent for music and sports.

This is another very important aspect of lymphoedema in children – struggling to come to terms with physical differences can be so much harder at a young age when it attracts unwelcome attention and prevents them from doing the things their friends can. They can find it hard to fit in, especially because their peers can occasionally be somewhat lacking in tact and kindness. At the age of seven, Rafael has already had to struggle to deal with his differences:

I am seven years old and I had 'water hands' when I was small. The other children at school ask all the time, 'Why

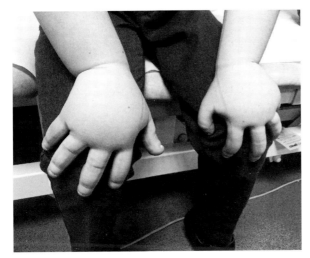

Hand swelling can cause functional problems, not to mention psychological issues. The swelling can affect grip strength and dexterity, making it difficult to do a variety of simple tasks such as hold a pen or do up buttons.

Rafael must wear his compression garments from morning until night to keep his swelling to a minimum.

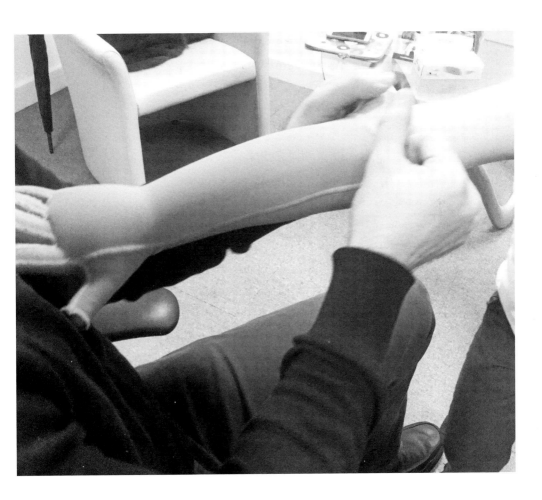

Rafael and Peter Mortimer at a check up (top) and at Wimbledon (bottom). Children with hand swelling are much more able to adapt to their disability than adults, so are able to do many activities such as playing sport.

do I have fat hands?' I keep telling them, my hands are not fat, they are swollen. They ask over and over again. This makes me sad. I tell them again and again they are not fat they are swollen. I ask mummy and daddy, 'Why do I have to be the one with fat hands?' It is not common but does make me special.

I have to wear gloves. I like colourful gloves and I choose crazy colours because it's cool. If I go to the toilet at school I take my gloves off but then the teachers have to help me put them back on again. It is very funny watching them struggle to put them back on. One day a new teacher asked me if I had cushioned gloves. They thought I had heat pads inside to keep my hands warm.

One day I came home from school with holes in my gloves and mummy asked 'Why have you got holes in your gloves?' and I said, 'Because I was hungry'. Mummy was very cross because I have to wait four months to get a new pair of gloves from the hospital.

My swollen hands mean I cannot do what the other boys and girls can do. I used to do gymnastics but I could not grip the bars properly or climb up the ropes like my friends could. That was sad for me because I like climbing ropes.

Writing is difficult because I find it hard to grip the pen. If I do too much writing my hands get tired and my skin can get red and sore. My teachers are going to get me to do touch-typing.

I play goalie in the school football team. I am able to punch the ball away more easily than my friends because I have big hands. My right leg is bigger than my left. If the football hits my leg it doesn't hurt so I use it to stop the ball going in the goal.

I like to use my first-aid kit to bandage my toy animals. My monkey had a broken tail so I put on the same three-layer bandage I have for my arms. I bandage my horse's two ill legs too and make them better.

My big hands bother me and I feel ugly and do not look nice. It's not fun or amusing but I make up for it with my brain and my kindness.

Hand swelling is difficult to hide and can have a serious effect on dexterity. When adults develop even mildly swollen hands, their ability to use them quickly declines, especially the ability to grip. Children, on the other hand, can adapt remarkably well, probably because they have never known anything different. Rafael's ability not only to hold a tennis racket but also to play tennis is inspiring. His mother named him after the great tennis player Rafael Nadal because she liked the name, but little did she know that her son would one day be able to play tennis, despite his lymphoedema – and even play on the courts at Wimbledon!

The problems children with lymphoedema face can continue into their teens – and arguably this can be the hardest time for a child to come to terms with the ways in which their condition makes them different. Arabella, who we met at the beginning of this chapter, is now fourteen and has extensive lymphoedema with swollen face, arms, body and legs. In these circumstances the condition produces a range of physical, psychological and social problems. The weight of her legs means that she cannot run around like other children. She also suffers serious infections that make her very ill and put her in hospital on a regular basis, meaning she misses school frequently.

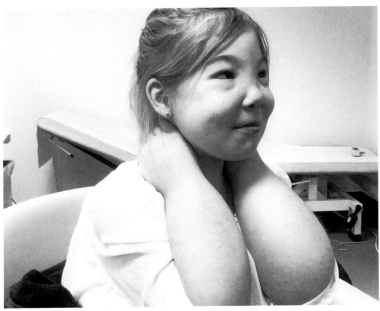

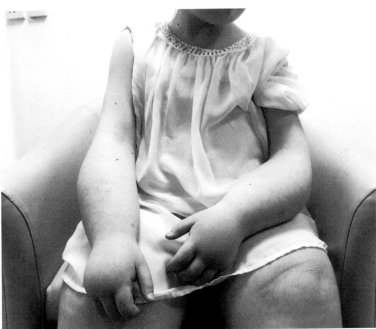

Arabella has swelling everywhere – face, eyes, hands, arms, feet and legs – because of the widespread faults in lymph drainage.

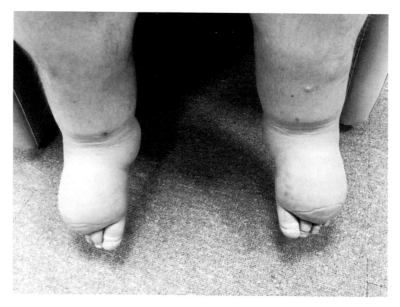

Foot swelling such as this is not only uncomfortable, making it very difficult to find shoes that fit, but also makes walking more difficult.

Her swollen limbs are disfiguring and attract unwelcome looks and unkind comments from other children and adults. And she struggles to find clothes and shoes that fit. Here is her story:

Hello my name is Bella Roberts and I have primary lymphoedema. Now I could just spend this whole page talking about what it is and how it is caused but that is just boring! I am going to talk about the real lymphoedema, the fun, the humorous and the sad stories of living with lymphoedema every day.

Let's start with the staring. Staring is a big issue in my life. Everywhere I go it seems like everyone wants to have a peek. Everyone tells me to just ignore it, but how can you when it happens every day; I hate it! Whenever someone stares I really have the urge to just go up to them and either punch them in the face or shout at them, but either of those two options could land me in a heap of trouble so I try to refrain from my urges.

My next issue is physical exercise. Now that's a struggle I deal with every day. To start with I stopped PE in year 9 because it was getting to the point where I couldn't handle it any more. I find physical exercise hard because of all the extra fluid I have to carry on top of my normal weight. To put it into more simple words it's like carrying fifty bricks on my legs, arms and all around my body. Missing PE isn't too bad because instead I get to go to the library and watch *Don't Tell the Bride*. However I make up for it by doing everyday exercises that other people find easy; for example, walking to school.

Next I am going to talk about the things that upset me. As I get ill quite a lot from infections I miss fun and impor- tant days at school or at home. For example, in year 9 I got an infection in my Hickman line *[a piece of sterile tubing inserted into a central body vein for blood access]*, which meant I had to be hospitalised for two weeks; I missed my little sister's first fashion show in her new secondary school, house events, fun lessons and just the latest gossip at school. Despite all these annoying things when I got out it was Easter holidays, so it wasn't all bad.

The next problem is clothes. Now that is a huge issue because I am swollen but also really short, so the clothes I have are either too tight or too long. Not to mention shoes – I get about one pair a year that fit my feet, each time having to go on a quest 'to the galaxy of H&M to find the shoe that will fit Cinderbella!' And if they don't look 'cool' – tough! I have to bear with it because all those Nikes just won't budge enough to fit my ginormous feet! I wear these same shoes for school, PE, going out, everything! So as you probably guess they sometimes don't even last a whole year. One day I am going to create a pair of shoes that can change shape to fit anyone's feet, but the way technology is going, they have probably already invented it.

To conclude, having lymphoedema isn't the best thing but it isn't the worst. It has its ups and downs, happy and sad moments but it's all ok in the end, I wouldn't change who I am for the world, but I would like more people to be aware of the condition because it is not very well known. My name is Bella Roberts and this is the real lymphoedema.

FAMILY LIFE

Arabella is not defined by her lymphoedema. It helps that she has the support of a strong family unit. Children dealing with the effects of lymphoedema need plenty of care, attention and assistance. But of course, this means that the condition has an impact on the whole family: on parents struggling to cope with their child's needs and treatment; on siblings who may at times feel neglected when their brother or sister's needs always take priority; and on the family as a whole when events such as holidays get disrupted by sudden illnesses and hospitalisations. All of this can take its toll. One mother shares the story of learning to cope with her son's condition:

Lymphoedema has been an interesting learning curve for us as a family but we have made the most of a difficult situation. We have dealt which each new challenge the condition has thrown our way, no matter how debilitating.

My son, George, was only four years old when he was diagnosed, five months after developing a very swollen left leg. We went from hospital to specialist up and down the country before we even heard the word 'lymphoedema'.

George is now nearly sixteen years old and unfortunately his lymphoedema has progressed for no known reason to involve his abdomen, genitals, and both legs and feet. He manages his lymphoedema, and bouts of cellulitis, as well as he can with various compression garments, MLD, prophylactic antibiotics, bandages, skin care and regular exercise.

We have overcome some very unpleasant and personal problems which George has had to face during his school years, and which he takes in his stride. It has certainly not stopped him and he always finds a solution when a challenge appears, with a fabulous circle of supportive friends as well as family. For example, George thoroughly enjoyed his first ski holiday four years ago and was looking forward to going again this year. However, unless we could find the time and money to have bespoke ski boots made (because his swollen feet did not fit in standard ski boots) – when he is also still growing – this was not going to be an option. George, being his usual determined self, proceeded to look into snowboarding instead of skiing and he is now enjoying a new sport without the need for bespoke boots. It's typical of his positive attitude to life. He can always find a way around a problem and he often acknowledges that there are always people in a more unfortunate situation.

I guess everyone reacts differently to having a child with lymphoedema. There was very little information out there either for children or parents so I began a journey to gain a better understanding of the condition. I have helped to organise events for children and teenagers with lymphoedema, and their families, so that they can support each other, as you can often feel isolated, and we have met many new friends in similar circumstances. Feedback from early events was amazing and they are now being organised nationally so families have a wider support group.

George's story is as much about his parents' journey as it is about his own. Adult patients complain about the difficulties of obtaining a diagnosis and the lack of information, but this can be even harder for parents, desperate to understand what is happening to their child. Recognising this, George and his mother raised substantial funds and produced a book for children with lymphoedema, called *The Big Book of Lymphoedema*. It received a British Medical Award and has had an impact worldwide after being translated into a number of other languages.

The book has brought hope and understanding to parents, and reassures them, and their children, that they are not alone. Credit to George's parents for helping so many others striving to find out anything they can on this otherwise neglected condition.

12

Other Forms of Lymphoedema

I n most cases, lymphoedema affects an arm or a leg but it can also affect any external part of the body such as the face, head and neck, torso and genitalia. Some of these can have a different cause and require a different approach to treatment, particularly as it is generally not possible to use compression garments and bandaging in such areas.

HEAD AND NECK

Lymphoedema of the head and neck has become more common due to the increasing incidence of head and neck cancer; for example, in the tongue or tonsils, the throat, voice box, salivary glands, or even in the nose or sinuses. Because such cancers can spread to either side of the neck, lymph glands are usually removed from both sides, and radiotherapy is often given on top, so lymph drainage can be affected in the whole area.

Where the lymph fluid collects can vary from one individual to another, although it is often in the lower part of the face and neck region, due to gravity. Sometimes it can be problematic around the eyes, which can make it difficult to open your eyelids in the morning, although this usually improves once you are up and about (as with other forms of lymphoedema, the use of facial muscles is important to keep the lymph flowing). In other cases the swelling can occur under the tongue, causing difficulties with chewing and eating, or under the chin, giving rise to a dewlap appearance rather like a bird's wattle.

Alastair is sixty years old and had been in perfect health until he developed throat cancer at the age of fifty-eight. He underwent both radiotherapy and chemotherapy but unfortunately within twelve months the cancer had returned. He then had to undergo extensive surgery, including removal of all of the lymph glands on one side of his neck. Within a matter of weeks he had developed considerable swelling in his left cheek extending up to his eye. Most of the swelling, however, was in the jowl area and under his chin. The inside of his mouth was also affected, which caused some difficulty with swallowing, speaking and breathing – symptoms that were always worse first thing on waking in the morning.

As he recovered from the surgery, the swelling became more of a problem. He was ready to go back to work as CEO of a major company but felt he could not do so because of his facial swelling and the difficulty speaking.

Alastair did find, however, that some simple measures had an immediate beneficial impact; raising the head of the bed overnight, for example, meant that the swelling on waking each morning was nowhere near as bad. He also embarked on a programme of specific facial exercises, KT and MLD, and soon his lymphoedema had improved to the point that he could return to work.

Lymphoedema swelling is more severe in the morning because lying down allows the fluid to pool more easily within your head and

'Lymphoedema. Yet another unpleasant symptom of cancer that affects so many people. We all have a family member or a friend who is either suffering, or has suffered from a cancer of some sort. It is an evil that must be fought and I sincerely pray that this book may help those with lymphoedema.'

Sir Cliff Richard

neck, and there is also a lack of movement in your facial muscles overnight. Everyone has a degree of swelling in their eyelids on waking, though most of us probably don't realise it as it's largely undetectable and the fluid drains away as soon as we have blinked a few times.

For anybody with lymphoedema involving the face or neck, using facial muscles is very important to stimulate lymph drainage. Exercises involving facial expressions such as frowning, lifting eyebrows, blinking, squeezing eyes shut, smiling, opening mouth wide, etc. are important aspects of treatment, particularly alongside other treatments such as KT and MLD (see pages 106 and 75).

FACIAL LYMPHOEDEMA DUE TO ROSACEA

Rosacea is a common condition affecting facial skin, causing redness due to enlarged skin blood vessels or 'broken blood vessels'.

People with fair skin are most often affected and can experience flushing, particularly in response to an increase in air temperature. With the redness often come red bumps and pimples, sometimes containing pus.

There is some evidence that the skin lymph vessels may be involved, and it can cause swelling of the face – but the problem doesn't affect the whole head and neck area, it appears only in the affected areas of the facial skin, such as the cheeks, forehead, nose and, in severe cases, the eyelids.

> Victor is thirty years old. Two years ago his forehead became red, as if he had been sunburnt, and the condition gradually worsened: the redness spread to his nose and cheeks; pimples came and went within the red areas; his face started to swell, and he noticed that his glasses left a big indentation on either side of his nose; and his eyelids became very puffy. The worst time was when he awoke in the morning. Some days he could not open his eyes properly because his eyelids were so full of fluid. He would have to delay going to work while he spent time pressing on his eyelids to squeeze the fluid out so he could open his eyes fully. He found his appearance embarrassing, especially when workmates would ask, 'What's happened to your face, Victor?'

The principles of treatment are: first to reduce inflammation through anti-acne antibiotics, and second, to improve lymph drainage along the same lines as for head and neck lymphoedema.

GENITAL LYMPHOEDEMA

Genital lymphoedema comes with its own special problems. It can be due to a genetic fault but more often than not it is caused by treatment of cancer of the male or female urogenital tract, for example the penis, vulva, cervix or prostate. Another cause is Crohn's disease, an inflammatory disorder of unknown cause, which usually affects the lower bowel, but sometimes can affect the skin of the external genitalia (anogenital granulomatosis or AGG).

While problems of a physical nature do arise with genital lymphoedema, such as difficulties emptying the bladder, it is usually problems of a psychological or sexual nature that cause the greatest distress. Charles developed lymphoedema from AGG and explains his experiences:

I first contracted genital lymphoedema approximately five years ago. I awoke one morning with an obviously swollen penis and, to some extent, scrotum. My first thought was that this had something to do with a recent twisted testicle but initial concern escalated to alarm when my GP had no idea what I was suffering from, and he referred me to a urologist.

The urologist took one look at me and exclaimed that I had lymphoedema. I was sent for an ultrasound, which highlighted nothing abnormal apart from the large amount of fluid, followed by a swathe of blood tests, which showed nothing untoward either. The doctor asked if I had tried squeezing the swelling to get it down. I hadn't for fear of making it worse but he implied that if I were to try this, the condition would simply go away.

Obviously the first thing you do these days when you have received a diagnosis is to Google it. After doing some detailed online research, which included some academic papers, it seemed the prognosis for genital lymphoedema was that there was no known cure, just management through horrendous-looking garments and regular massage.

At first I tortured myself, going over and over the thought that if I had just stopped sleeping on my front after the testicle twist, this would not have happened. I also thought that there was simply no point getting a second opinion – my internet research seemed to corroborate what the doctor had said, and there was no information on a cure.

So began the next five years of managing my condition as best I could. Most of the writing on genital lymphoedema management is around undergarments that help prevent the build-up of fluid through gravity. I find any garment that keeps my scrotum nearer my body extremely uncomfortable, largely due to heat, sweatiness and itchiness. I have to find jeans and trousers for work with increased space in the 'gusset' to allow some freedom of movement. Tracksuit pants are the order of the day as soon as I am at home.

Some of the other hurdles that have befallen me include the thankfully rare bouts of infection which strike. In one particular situation a small, day-long workshop was made quite excruciating, which was probably the result of sitting uncomfortably on a train for three and a half hours without the freedom to 'adjust' myself to a more comfortable position. I have changed jobs since, which has reduced my need to travel, and the infections have been limited to four at the most.

Directional peeing is also a challenge. Urinals are better than toilets but I constantly have to dry clean my trousers. You also spend far more time cleaning up after yourself.

Thankfully, I was married at the time of contracting this condition and have a wonderful, fully supportive wife. However, I was concerned when the time came for us to try for our first child – there was often a lot of increased heat in my scrotum and I was worried that it would affect the quality of my sperm. Thankfully, our child was born healthy so those initial concerns have been overcome and we are now trying for number two.

I suppose I can't continue without mentioning sex. The biggest impact here has been the inability to have spontaneous sex, as I need to squeeze the fluid away beforehand otherwise the experience is uncomfortable for us both. This has not had such a big impact as it may have done prior to children but it does mean that there has to be some planning, which is not ideal. Again, I have been so lucky with the understanding of my wife. I suppose I can admit this when speaking anonymously, but I was always quite pleased with my penis. I have female friends that complain of the inherent ugliness of the male member but I always felt that mine was okay in that department in terms of size, straightness etc. That has obviously now been lost and at some point, as my new-found treatment continues, it looks like surgery will be required to help some of the issues outlined above.

Charles underwent successful surgery to reduce the size of his penis and scrotum. Surgery is particularly useful for treating genital lymphoedema at an early stage because the usual treatment of massage, compression garments and exercise do not tend to be effective.

LIPOEDEMA

Fat or 'tree trunk' legs may be due to lymphoedema but they can also be caused by a condition called lipoedema. It causes swelling mainly due to fat rather than fluid, but not because of regular obesity. It has been included here for two reasons: first, it is frequently mistaken for lymphoedema; second, it can develop into lymphoedema and therefore its origins may have something to do with the lymph system.

Lipoedema appears to be almost exclusive to women. From puberty or at times of hormonal change, for example after pregnancy or even at menopause, excessive fat is deposited on the hips, buttocks, thighs and legs. Sometimes the arms can become larger as well, but the body (above the belly button), head, neck, hands and feet remain unaffected, so the lower half of the body is disproportionately larger.

Unlike obesity the fat involved in lipoedema does not respond to diet, but as far as we know the fat is no different in composition. Dieting results in loss of fat from the rest of the body, but with little or no change to the area affected by lipoedema. The affected areas can also be painful and tender, unlike in lymphoedema. Those affected by lipoedema often complain that even the slightest knock on their legs causes pain and that they bruise easily. And if lymphoedema also develops (lipoedema-lymphoedema syndrome), it can complicate the problem, adding large quantities of fluid to already swollen, heavy limbs.

The cause of lipoedema is not known. There is often a family history – the mother or a grandmother is usually affected – which suggests it is an inherited genetic cause. The fact that men appear unaffected also suggests a hormonal influence but no hormonal abnormalities have ever been found.

The condition can present a challenge for everyday activities, and the fact that the fat won't respond to diet can be particularly frustrating when undiagnosed – which it often is, as it's not very well known in the medical profession and is frequently mistaken for obesity, or occasionally lymphoedema. Penelope shares her experience of the condition:

> I am a thirty-one-year-old female and I have had problems with my legs from puberty. During my teens my legs never had the same appearance or shape as other girls', which was particularly noticeable during PE lessons. I loved participating in sport at school but I was often ridiculed and bullied for being overweight even though I wasn't fat, except in my legs.
>
> I competed in dressage to a high level (I was lucky, a great sport for me as the horse didn't care what I looked like!), but I remember the embarrassment shopping for long riding boots to fit my enormous 18-inch calves. The XXXL boots had to be specially imported and even then they didn't fit properly and taking them off was a near impossible task! Other members of my family have always been keen on exercise, so apart from my love of horses I was encouraged to join them in the gym, where there are all shapes and sizes, but it didn't have any effect on my legs.

I started eating less as I thought a restricted diet would cure my grotesque legs but it made little difference and instead I developed an eating disorder.

In 2014 I lost three stone for my brother's wedding, through excessive exercise and an extreme diet of less than 1,000 calories; I was determined to be a thin bridesmaid. The weight fell off the top half of my body to the point that I looked wasted, but my legs never changed size or shape. They just remained the same. My feet looked normal but my lower legs above my ankles were huge and my grandmother called them 'cankles' (chunky ankles). While the rest of my body looked toned my legs and thighs were wobbly with terrible cellulite. They were also quite tender even with the gentlest of knocks.

Clothes shopping has no pleasure, mainly disappointment. Finding jeans is a constant battle. I am tall, and measure a size 12/14 on the top and a size 18 on the bottom; I'm just not the right shape for the high street! I currently have one pair of unfashionable jeans that I will wear until they fall apart. One day I'd like to find a trendy pair of skinny jeans that actually go over my calves!

I became frustrated. I was constantly being told that it was just stubborn fat that would shift in the end so I exercised even more, but there was no change. Sadly, my legs have never made me feel attractive and this has affected my relationship with men. I have only had a couple of boyfriends that ended badly. My legs being an object of derision, my self-esteem and confidence are always left shattered.

I started to realise there could be a problem and that it was more than just a weight issue; after all I was

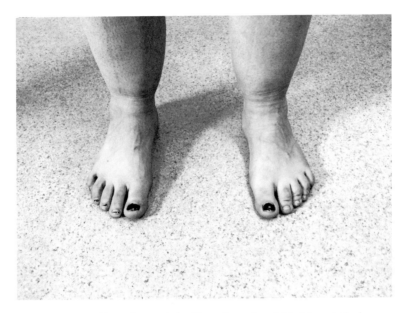

A 'fat' ankle or 'cankle' is characteristic of lipoedema. Extra fat builds up in the lower leg immediately above the ankle bones, while the rest of the foot remains normal.

still thin except for my legs. After reading an article in a national newspaper on lipoedema I made an appointment to see my GP. Unfortunately, I had to go back several times before I was referred to a specialist, as they had never even heard of the condition. But eventually I was referred on to a doctor who confirmed that yes I did have lipoedema. What a relief! I had a reason for my 'tree trunk' legs and I wasn't fat!

Even since my diagnosis, I have still experienced prejudice. I have often been asked if I've tried diet and exercise. It can be really hard to stay positive. There still seems to be a lot of stigma attached to having lipoedema.

It has been difficult and has required perseverance, but exercise has been my saviour. I go to the gym regularly and

I have a fantastic personal trainer to keep me motivated. My philosophy is no matter how much my legs hurt, never give up, and believe me they are heavy, ache and I constantly suffer knee and hip pain, but it is the exercise which has controlled my fat legs.

I recently competed at the British national indoor rowing championships in the women's relay team, winning gold, which was a huge achievement. It took a tremendous amount of effort as my legs felt heavy and the pain in my calves was unbearable, but I did it! I hope to return with my teammates to defend the title later in the year. No matter how unrealistic exercise seems, it really does help and I refuse to let lipoedema dictate my life.

One of the problems with lipoedema is that although the condition itself is not obesity, the larger limbs can make exercise hard, and people can gain weight more easily. This type of additional fat will respond to diet but not the lipoedema. Exercise can help by improving muscle tone and strength but it really has to be of almost Olympic proportions as in Penelope's story. Not surprisingly, sufferers of lipoedema easily become discouraged.

The definitive treatment for lipoedema is liposuction, but that should not be tried unless fitness levels are good and any additional obesity has been addressed.

LYMPHOEDEMA OF THE GUT

There is one, much more unusual, lymphatic condition, which occurs when there are abnormalities in the gut, where special lymph vessels (known as lacteals) absorb dietary fat through the lining of the small bowel. One of the major functions of the lymph system is fat absorption from the gut, so if drainage is disrupted here, it can cause specific problems: bouts of tummy pain and diarrhoea, as well as a loss of protein and other valuable nutrients into the bowel with the body's other waste. The medical term for a failure of the lymph system within the digestive tract is intestinal lymphangiectasia, which is usually associated with lymphoedema.

Diet is therefore extremely important in managing and alleviating the symptoms, as dietician Rani Nagarajah explains in relation to one of her patients:

Daniel was born with his left leg longer than his right. At the age of seven his left thigh began to swell. By his teens, fluid had built up in the whole of his left leg and his penis. Fat containing lymph, which had not been absorbed properly from the gut, was diverted to other parts of the lymph system such as the leg and genitalia, where it would leak out of his skin. Daniel would find this embarrassing because it would look as if he had wet himself. He was also prone to getting cellulitis, which would make him feel very ill, very quickly, and he suffered from frequent tummy pain and explosive diarrhoea. Fatty meals like a cheese-burger made the leakage and diarrhoea much worse. The symptoms interfered with his social life and relationships during his teens and then with his job when he left school. Daniel now works as a roofer and the constant bending and crouching made him feel uncomfortable and made the leaking worse.

In 2012 a MRI scan showed a large misshapen mass of lymph vessels in his left pelvis and thigh, close to his bladder, which was causing the problem. What fat he absorbed found its way into these abnormal lymph vessels and then flowed in reverse to the skin of his genitals and foot. The size and location of the vessels meant that it would be too difficult for a surgeon to remove, so he had to visit a dietician to customise a low-fat diet to compensate for the failure of the gut lymph system to absorb fat.

As Daniel has a very physical job, it was important to compensate for the loss of energy from fat by adding extra protein and carbohydrate. Within a few weeks his diarrhoea stopped and all leaking had dried up. Furthermore his lymphoedema swelling improved as he was now absorbing protein properly. His mood and energy levels also improved.

Around the time of his thirtieth birthday, Daniel relaxed his diet and ate fatty foods for several days in a row. He immediately noticed a recurrence of diarrhoea and leaking of lymph from his toes. He now follows his strict low-fat diet six days a week but treats himself to a roast dinner or a pizza on a Sunday. This helps to ensure that there is no leaking and gives him good control over his bowels on workdays. He still experiences some gut problems on Sundays but feels that it is a price worth paying. He has not had any episodes of cellulitis since he started his diet, and feels he is no longer held back by the condition, as he explains:

Growing up with lymphoedema was a total nightmare! I used to pray every day for a cure or that someone would just kill me. I used to think my life was over. I would never go on holiday with my friends because I would never wear shorts – I was afraid I would get called a freak and everyone would point at me! And I never had a girlfriend because I didn't think anyone would want to go out with a freak like me. Every time I went to the hospital I was always hoping for good news. And sometimes I would break down in tears because I didn't get what I was hoping for.

Then something amazing happened! I found that going to the gym and running a lot and eating the right food not only made me feel so much better about myself but actually helped with the swelling of my leg. The more I run, the smaller the swelling seems to get. And the compression stocking and shorts made a big difference as well. I couldn't do the things I do without them. I've been able to do so much and achieved so many goals I wanted – I went travelling round Thailand for two months; went bungee jumping; sky diving; wing-walking; completed a 'tough mudder' (a 12-mile, 26-obstacle race); a Reebok Spartan race of 15 miles and 68 obstacles; and my biggest achievement was a Rat Race – 20 miles and 200 obstacles. That was so hard. But I just keep pushing myself. I can do anything any normal person can! My condition never holds me back now.

A faulty lymph system affecting the digestive tract is considered rare but may occur more often than realised. It is difficult to diagnose and would probably not be considered at all if it were not for the presence of lymphoedema.

Most of these forms of lymphoedema are not as well known as when the condition occurs in the arm or leg, partly because they are less common. However, there is another type of lymphoedema that most people have never heard of, but that affects millions of people around the world: filariasis.

13

Lymphoedema Worldwide

We briefly touched on the occurrence of lymphoedema in other parts of the world in Chapter 3. There are two main causes in particular: lymphatic filariasis and podoconiosis, both recognised by the World Health Organisation as neglected tropical diseases.

LYMPHATIC FILARIASIS OR ELEPHANTIASIS

Dr S. R. Narahari is chairman and director of the Institute of Applied Dermatology (IAD) in Kerala, India. Here he describes the very different challenges presented by lymphoedema when it is caused by lymphatic filariasis:

Lymphatic filariasis is an infection caused by a mosquito: an infected mosquito bites a human and deposits microscopic larvae (microfilaria) into the skin. The larvae migrate to the nearest lymph vessel in the unsuspecting human, and then on to the bigger lymph vessels close to the lymph glands where they mature into adult worms. They mate and form worm nests, which physically block the flow of lymph within the vessel, and so lymphoedema starts. Not all people infected with lymphatic filariasis develop lymphoedema, but when they do the swelling can be so severe, and the skin changes so marked, it is called 'elephantiasis'.

People are only affected by filariasis in regions with infected mosquitos and that means a tropical country. Arguably India has more cases of lymphoedema than any other country on the planet because of the high numbers of cases of lymphatic filariasis.

As well as swelling, the disease also causes frequent fevers as the body fights the worm infection. Eventually the fevers cease, when the worms die, but by then the lymph system has likely been permanently damaged. Then the fevers might start again but this time due to bacterial infection. This is now just the same as with any form of lymphoedema, where the sufferer develops recurrent bouts of bacterial infection, equivalent to cellulitis but called acute dermato-lymphangio-adenitis or ADLA. With each episode of infection the swelling gets worse, often reaching gigantic proportions.

In one case we saw Mr Muhammed Shaban, a twenty-year-old plumber from Thana, Mumbai. He had filarial lymphoedema of both lower limbs, which developed over four years before he accessed any treatment.

The swelling had started with an episode of high fever and gradually oedema extended up one leg, reaching his thigh. He then had an injury resulting in a chronic wound on his leg, which did not respond to conventional treatments and started to emit a foul smell. Sometime later he experienced multiple bouts of fever and abscesses formed in his groin. With each episode of bacterial infection his leg got even bigger.

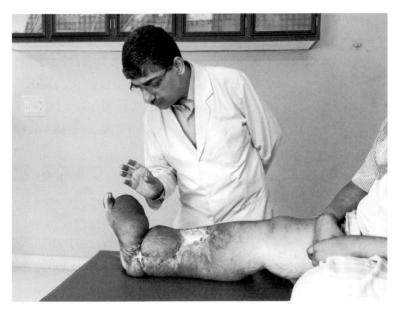

Dr Narahari at the Institute of Applied Dermatology in Kerala explaining lymphoedema, and its proposed treatment, to a patient.

Over the next four months he started getting severe knee-joint pain, which affected his mobility. Despite his young age, he started using a walking stick to move around. He was severely distressed by both the disability and foul-smelling ulcer. He had to depend on his mother to look after him and he had to give up his job. He thought there was no hope in his life.

He knew he had lymphoedema because people in his community had told him – it is common in that area. He heard about services for lymphoedema treatment through word of mouth from a treated patient and attended the IAD clinic in Kerala even though it was many miles away from his home and it was a difficult journey to get there. When he arrived the staff saw that one leg was hugely swollen and had multiple ulcers, which were discharging foul smelling pus. A nurse counsellor explained lymphatic filariasis to him and his mother as the cause of all his problems, and what he could expect from the programme of treatment.

He was put on a course of antibiotics. The ulcers were dressed with Ayurvedic medicines. The intact skin was treated with Ayurvedic creams. Indian massage was administered as well as leg bandaging and yoga exercises. The patient, his mother and other family members who attended were instructed on how to continue care once he was back home. His treatment lasted twenty-one days, by which time the ulcers were healed, the odour had gone and the swelling was markedly reduced.

He continued his treatment at home with little assistance from his family members. He was able to attend his second follow up at the outpatient clinic without a walking stick as his leg was much smaller and less heavy. The knee joint pain completely went away and thus his mobility improved. He was now integrating back into society and felt much less stigmatised. He had no further infections or fevers after the treatment. He returned to his job as a plumber part time and once again was earning his living on his own.

In Kasaragod, in Kerala, in southern India, the IAD is devoted to improving the management of lymphoedema. The clinic started in 1999 and started to develop new treatments integrating Indian Ayurvedic practices with Western methods. Ayurveda literally means 'life knowledge' and is the use of traditional medicines and techniques. Most healthcare centres in India use some form of Ayurvedic medicine as people see it as more acceptable and so are more likely to stick to the treatment.

There is limited public funding for medical care in India so the clinic not only provided the treatment for Muhammed but also raised the sponsorship to cover 90 per cent of his treatment costs.

In order to reach out to all communities, the IAD has created lymphoedema treatment camps, which take place in outlying rural villages. Each camp has a patient education class, a skincare demonstration and a yoga and exercise class. Skin disease is very common in India because of the heat and poorer living conditions and sanitation, which means a much higher risk of cellulitis in lymphoedema, hence why skin care is so important.

Patients and their families are taught to wash the skin twice a day with soap and water. For more intensive cleaning, soaking solutions made from boiling fine powders of particular medicine plants are used. Massage with herbal oil is taught to encourage lymph drainage, but any very infected skin areas may be treated with modern drugs. Compression bandaging is also taught.

A treatment programme that employs locally available supervisors and simple technology that is easy to administer and teach has been successful. Most importantly, it is low cost and can be delivered to rural communities.

Lymphatic filariasis can be eliminated through preventive chemotherapy with single doses of two medicines for people living in areas where the infection is present. In 2000 the World Health Organisation established the Global Programme to Eliminate Lymphatic Filariasis (GPELF). This has resulted in the prevention, or cure, of more than 97 million cases of lymphatic filariasis. There is still a lot of work to do, particularly in India, to eradicate this neglected tropical disease, but even if new cases are prevented those already affected with filarial lymphoedema will be around for many years to come.

PODOCONIOSIS
(NON-FILARIAL ELEPHANTIASIS)

There is another form of lymphoedema called podoconiosis, caused by silicate particles entering the skin from barefoot walking during childhood. Once again the swelling and skin changes resemble elephant skin so podoconiosis is also called 'non-filarial elephantiasis'. It affects people mainly in tropical and sub-tropical regions, and has occurred in fifteen countries across Africa, Central America and Asia. Dr Claire Fuller, Chair of the International Foundation for Dermatology, is a consultant dermatologist who has developed a research interest in tropical dermatology and in particular podoconiosis.

Podoconiosis, also known as 'podo' or sometimes as 'mossy foot' due to its appearance, is a tropical lower-limb lymphoedema, which is caused by the combination of a genetic predisposition and regular exposure to irritant minerals in the soil. It occurs mainly in farmers living in the tropical highlands such as Ethiopia, who work their land barefoot.

It is thought that the mineral particles contained in these fertile soils pass through the skin and into the lymph vessels. These particles then irritate the lining of the lymph vessels leading to scarring and narrowing, and eventually blockage, of these channels so that they are no longer able to carry lymph away from the feet and legs, leading to progressive swelling. It is further evidence of why skin and foot care are so important in both preventing and treating lymphoedema.

Once the condition has developed, the person is more susceptible to bacterial infections and episodes of fever, as happens with all forms of lymphoedema.

The Mossy Foot clinic in Soddo, Ethiopia, treats people suffering from the condition, and that is where I met Bethsaida. She wore a haunting expression of hopelessness, and wasn't even sure why she had come to the clinic. She was twenty and had been suffering from podoconiosis for about five years. The swelling of her legs had worsened over those years, especially after every acute attack, which was accompanied by fever and increased swelling. Patients suffering from these attacks are completely incapacitated and bed-ridden for a few days. During an early infection Bethsaida had taken a course of antibiotics but she could ill-afford the cost of these and so during subsequent episodes simply had to wait for the flu-like symptoms to subside without medication.

By the time she attended the clinic, she was suffering acute attacks twice a month; they seemed to be triggered when she was getting the produce ready from the family small holding for market day. Even between episodes she had heavy, large, swollen legs, too big to be able to wear shoes, ugly to look at and studded with skin lumps. The hard lumps or nodules had come on gradually; they ranged in size from 2–4 cm across and were very woody and hard.

Podoconiosis can be completely prevented if individuals with the genetic risk avoid frequent barefoot contact with the soil. If they wear shoes from childhood, the condition will not develop. Once established, it is challenging but not impossible to improve the situation. A simple regimen of washing the skin of the feet and lower legs daily, moisturising the skin once it has been carefully dried, donning socks (or if possible compression stockings) and then shoes can have a significant benefit. Shoes not only protect the foot from further exposure to the harmful soil but also limit the swelling of the feet during the day.

At the clinic, Root, one of the 'podo agents', led Bethsaida to the newcomer's area. A podo agent is a previous patient who uses the knowledge they have gained through their own experiences to help others who need treatment. Root had followed the simple treatment plan and was now better. She was delighted to support the clinics and gave back a day per week of her time to welcome new patients and encourage them to participate in the treatment that had transformed her life so dramatically three years earlier.

Root explained the basics of the simple treatment, showing Bethsaida how to wash the leg and foot, to dry the skin carefully, especially between the toes, and to apply a greasy moisturiser to the skin of the lower leg, foot and toes. Once this had soaked in, Bethsaida was given a pair of clean socks and then some shoes that had been selected to fit her swollen and misshapen foot. Root also shared her own experience of how within a month of starting this daily treatment, the acute attacks that had punctuated her life so destructively stopped completely, as did the accompanying bacterial odour. Watching Bethsaida's expression change from despair to hope as she listened to Root's encouragement was a very moving experience.

After three months of treatment, Bethsaida's swelling had reduced to the extent that she was able to wear ordinary trainers rather than the custom-made boots that were the only thing that fitted her feet at the start of her treatment.

Podoconiosis is not only an uncomfortable illness, it is also massively stigmatising. The folds of the thickened skin become home to bacteria that generate an unpleasant odour, and this leads to patients' social isolation from families and friends. Before attending the clinic, Bethsaida was no longer permitted to eat at the same time as her family as they found the smell so hard to cope with. She was ostracised.

When I first visited the area, I learned that we were not able to go to the patients' homes as the project car was well known and our presence would identify the family as a 'podo' household. This was something that they all kept secret, as it would limit marriage options. The risk of being seen also prevented those affected from being able to join social gatherings.

Fortunately there is a positive end to this story; some of the treatment programmes have really focused on community education and myth debunking. In areas with a high incidence of podo, project workers have gone into schools, churches and mosques to raise awareness and teach the community about the disease – how it is not possible to 'catch' it, and how it is not caused by a curse or other spiritual activity. Over the decade of their activities I have seen changes in community attitudes. On my last visit to the area, strangers would approach the project team in public places and show their legs to see if they might have early podoconiosis.

At another clinic I attended, I was introduced to Aykale, another podo agent, and shoemaker, who helps out her local community and has seen a huge difference in attitudes. She was expecting about 200 patients to attend this particular monthly event. Once everyone had arrived she began to tell her story. She told us she started to get symptoms when she was about twenty; her mother and brother also had podo. Her father had left the family when her mother developed symptoms soon after Aykale was born. They never saw him again. The family were taken in by a local church, which provided food and shelter for them. She realised she was very lucky to have this support but aspired to a better, independent life.

Coming from a podo family, she had been too embarrassed to attend school and so had no formal education. Once her symptoms had started she also knew she had little chance of ever being married as no one wanted a podo patient as a life partner. She started to try to make a living by collecting and selling avocados, but the selling days usually triggered a painful acute attack with fever, resulting in incapacitation for several days so she had so stop.

She then heard about the Mossy Foot projects and started to come to her area clinic. Once she had shown she was able to stick to the skin care regimen effectively, she was provided with suitable subsidised shoes. Some time later, having improved even further, she was no longer having any acute attacks and her skin texture had virtually returned to normal.

She trained as a shoemaker to help make the bespoke shoes needed for the new patients with enlarged feet and limbs. She became so fast at making the shoes, she usually completed her weekly quota (set by her employers, the Podoconiosis Project) by Thursday. She could then spend Friday and Saturday running her own stall in the market, making, mending and cleaning shoes, so enabling her to supplement her income. She also saved enough money to be able to rent a small room in which she could live safely and support her mother. The message from a fellow patient sharing the impact of successful treatment on her life is very powerful, and can encourage others to seek help and make a positive change in their lives.

Sometimes all it takes are small steps to make all the difference in transforming the lives of sufferers of filariasis and podoconiosis. But the first and most important step – across the world – is raising awareness of lymphoedema: making sure sufferers know about preventative measures and treatments; educating others so that sufferers are not stigmatised; and attracting funding so that even more can be done to help people living with the condition.

Conclusion: Hope

R eaders will perhaps not be cheered by some of the themes of this book: the delayed diagnoses; the problems encountered by victims of lymphoedema; the somewhat outdated treatments; and the distressing stories of patients suffering from grotesque swelling in underdeveloped countries.

The truth is that medical conditions grab headlines only if they are fatal, or if there have been significant new advances in medical or surgical management. Lymphoedema is a chronic long-term condition. It has been known about for centuries, long before diseases such as diabetes were discovered, yet not one drug has been developed to treat the condition; there is no simple diagnostic test to confirm its presence; and new microsurgical techniques are only just becoming available. If lymphoedema is to claim the spotlight and capture the interest of clinicians, what is needed is a breakthrough test or a novel form of treatment.

This is where our hope lies. In recent years, research scientists have started to discover a whole new world of information regarding the lymph system and its role in various diseases, not least lymphoedema. The great breakthrough has been in the field of genetics, establishing which genes are responsible for the growth and function of the lymph system. Some of the genes that cause lymphoedema have also been identified and so can be used to increase our understanding of how they cause the condition. Further investigation of these genes should, in time, enable new treatments to be developed, perhaps even ones that could reverse the condition, rather than just managing the symptoms.

This has already been achieved in animals. For example, proteins responsible for growing lymph vessels have been successfully given to animals with lymphoedema, and have shown an improvement in the number and quality of the lymph vessels, and in the swelling. Drugs have also worked in reducing inflammation in animals, based on the idea that an imbalance of immune cells in the body can contribute to inflammation, leading to lymphoedema. This approach has already led to breakthroughs in treating a number of conditions, such as rheumatoid arthritis and multiple sclerosis.

Much work remains to be done to bring these approaches to the clinical arena but drug trials in humans with lymphoedema have now started. So there is hope, and exciting times lie ahead as science advances ever closer to the breakthroughs necessary to conquer lymphoedema.

Appendix 1: Exercises

The non-weight-bearing environment of water can be especially helpful for lymphoedema. For centuries the healing power of water has been used in many forms and there is no doubt that the benefits it provides are considerable. Stretching and moving in water provides support, comfort and resistance all at the same time, allowing you to develop both your flexibility and strength.

The following exercises were developed by Gemma Levine to help with the lymphoedema in her arm, inspired by a Swedish technique called Mensedick, and approved by remedial exercise specialist Jon Bowskill. They are good examples of how movement within water can be used to help improve the lymph circulation, as well as improve mobility, cardiovascular health, circulation, relaxation, energy plus overall health and well-being.

As with any form of new exercise it is important to get the green light from your doctor first. You should begin the exercises slowly and carefully with close attention to your technique, stopping if you have any adverse symptoms, aches or pains.

Remember, let your swollen limb tell you what exercise it likes and doesn't like!

POOL EXERCISES

Exercise 1

Exercise 3a

Exercise 3b

Exercise 3c

Exercise 3d

1. Deep breathing. Sit, straight back, legs apart. Hands on bent knees. Breathe in slowly, hold breath in for count of 5. Breathe out slowly and repeat 10 times.

2. Swim for 20 minutes in your favoured style. Be careful not to strain your neck if using breast stroke.

3. Go to side of pool or to a bar at side of pool, water level to be above waist.

   a) Hold on with both hands and raise feet on to ball of foot and then down, slowly, not quite touching the floor of the pool. Repeat 24 times, exercising foot and calf muscles.

   b) Hold on with both hands, draw knees up to chest and down 20 times, stretching the spine.

   c) Hold on to bar with right hand. Rotate left leg 5 times and then again in the opposite direction. Repeat with right leg. Exercises hip joints.

   d) Hold on to bar with both hands. One knee slightly bent close to bar and other leg stretched out behind with toe (not heel) on base of floor of the pool. Stretch calf muscles to count of 12. Then repeat with the other leg.

e) Hold on to the bar, grasp right ankle and pull up and firmly back, drawing the heel towards the buttock. Hold for a count of 10. Repeat with the left leg. Stretches thighs.

Exercise 3e

f) Lift right knee up to chest, as far as possible to stretch back thigh. Hold for a count of 12. Repeat with the left leg.

Exercise 3f

4. Find a corner. Place arms outstretched to hold on to both corners (or bar) of the wall of the pool.

Exercise 4a

a) Rise up to the top of the water surface on your back. Place both knees together and swing from left to right 20 times, to strengthen obliques.

Exercise 4a

b) Draw legs up to chest then kick one leg forward and back ten times and then repeat with the other leg, 10 times. Finally both legs together 10 times. Kick with as much strength as you can. Good for circulation of lower limbs and strengthening muscles around knee joints.

Exercise 4b

c) Draw both legs up and exercise a scissor movement, crossing legs over one another, 20 times. When finished, kick legs vigorously

Exercise 4b

Exercise 4c

Exercise 5

Exercise 6

Exercise 7a

Exercise 7b

Exercise 7c

Exercise 7c

to lower to the floor of the pool. Exercises the inner thighs.

5. Go to the deep end and tread water 200 times (100 times for each leg) with elbows and wrists above water, hands loosely clenched. This is a difficult exercise and can only be achieved with practice and time. You might only be able to do 5 or 10 at the beginning. Strengthens stomach muscles.

6. If there are steps: hold on to a rail or the side and place your feet on a step at waist level. Push forwards and backwards, bending knees, 20 times. Strengthens spine and knees joints.

7. Stand with water above waist level.

    a) Rotate one shoulder forwards 5 times, then backwards 5 times. Repeat with the other shoulder. Strengthens shoulder muscles.

    b) Rotate head to the right, then to the left, 5 times. Exercises neck.

    c) With both arms at the same time, clench fists, rotate arms 'out' and then 'in', 8 times. Rotate both wrists left and right 5 times each way. Then hold your hands as if praying, push gently down to the left and then the right,

8 times. Then the same with the thumbs, pressing the top inner soft part of the thumb hard against each other, 8 times. Finish by shaking wrists vigorously.

Exercise 7c

d) Finish this exercise, by tightly gripping your hands behind your back and pulling in your shoulder blades firmly, elbows nearly touching. Release and repeat 10 times. Exercise chest muscles.

Exercise 7d

8. Stand in the water so that your shoulders are submerged.

Exercise 8a

a) Sweep your arms forwards and backwards using your hands as paddles.

Exercise 8a

b) As you sweep your arms keep your tummy tight and try not to let your body sway back and forth too much. Repeat 20 times.

Exercise 8a, aerial

9. Stand in the water so that your shoulders are submerged.

Exercise 8a, aerial

a) Lift your shoulders up and forwards.

b) As your shoulders reach the top of the shrug position roll them back squeezing the shoulder blades together before returning to the start and repeating. Repeat 10 times.

Exercise 9a

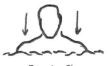

Exercise 9b

Exercise 10a

10. Stand in the water so that your shoulders are submerged, holding a float in front of you with your palms facing.

a) Holding your tummy in tight, try to sweep the water away to your right side with the float. You should keep your chest up throughout and concentrate on the rotation coming from your trunk as you move.

Exercise 10b

b) Sweep the float back to the centre. There should be equal effort moving the float away from your centre as back to the start.

Exercise 10c

c) Repeat, this time sweeping the water away to your left side, and then bring it back to the centre again. Repeat 10 times.

Exercise 11a

11. Submerge yourself so that the water comes up to your sternum.

a) Stride forward purposefully.

b) As you move your legs, work your palms through the water at the same time, extending the opposite arm to the leg you are using.

Exercise 11b

c) Keep your tummy tight and maintain good upright posture throughout. Repeat for 100 strides.

12. Finally, return to the steps.

a) Lift one leg on to a step higher than the waist and with a straight leg, push down at the knee 8 times, then the other leg. Strengthens back, calf and knees.

Exercise 12a

b) On step 3, crouch (squat) with knees bent and rise up and down in a bobbing movement, 30 times. Strengthen thighs, ham strings and knees.

Exercise 12b

c) Sit on step and clench your buttock muscles tightly and then release 10 times.

Exercise 12c

d) Repeat deep breathing exercises from exercise 1, at the start of the course. This will enable you to relax before leaving.

Exercise 12d

Of course, not every case will be the same and some patients may need to have a programme tailored to their own needs. It is important that you start slowly and as the weeks go by, as you get stronger, gradually build up on the counts. Always, one extra for luck!

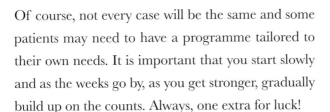

Illustrations by Rikki Marr

Appendix 2: Nutrition

There is no clear evidence that lymphoedema sufferers need different guidelines on nutrition to anyone else. But it is more important that they do adopt a healthy approach to their diet because, alongside exercise, it is key to losing the excess weight that can exacerbate their condition. Dietician Rani Nagarajah looks at some aspects of nutrition that can help make a difference:

1. Enjoy a balanced diet: the Eatwell Plate which is promoted on the NHS website is a good basis for a diet plan. It recommends a balance between protein, carbohydrates and fat, and promotes fresh, natural products like vegetables, fruit, nuts, seeds and beans, rather than processed ones. It also recommends eating a wide range of foods.

2. Reduce your salt intake: the modern diet tends to contain higher levels of salt than our bodies need, and can have a number of health consequences, and too much salt can exacerbate fluid retention.

3. Manage your carbohydrates: if you give yourself a sudden carbohydrate hit - e.g. take away foods, pastries, pizzas, cakes, biscuits, sweets – then your body needs to send a quick rush of insulin to deal with it. We know the diabetic dangers associated

with this but one of the main actions of insulin is to expand blood vessels leading to the likelihood of increased swelling.

4. Maintain a good supply of fluids: it is a huge temptation to reduce water consumption when you are already feeling a fluid overload, but your body needs water to keep things like salt flushed out through our kidneys. When you drink a glass of water, it does not go to your ankles.

5. Restrict your alcohol intake. There are four negative aspects to alcohol intake: it is very, very calorific; it makes you hungry; it disinhibits you so you have less control over what you eat; and alcohol makes blood vessels expand – hence the pink cheeks – and so become more leaky therefore making it more likely that ankles and hands will swell.

6. Eat more spicy food: there is some evidence to show that spices, including chilli, can increase your metabolic rate. However, it is unlikely that eating spicy food will lead to large amounts of weight loss. Other factors, particularly your total calorie intake and activity levels, are more important.

7. Caffeine can help: it can fractionally stimulate your metabolism and help you exercise more effectively – a double espresso can increase resting energy expenditure by up to 10 per cent for three hours.

8. Eat little and more often: this may help you feel less hungry, meaning you are less likely to gorge or overeat later in the day. Try a healthy snack such as a portion of fruit in between your meals.

These are just a few suggestions; after all there are whole books on how to lose weight and no simple solution. What works for one person may not work for another. The important thing is to combine a nutritious diet with exercise.

Resources

Organisations such as the Lymphoedema Support Network (LSN), a registered charity set up in 1991 in the UK, play an important role in educating and supporting patients with the condition by providing a high standard of information and promoting self-help.

Lymphoedema Support Network
St. Luke's Crypt, Sydney Street, London SW3 6NH, UK
Email: adminlsn@lymphoedema.freeserve.co.uk
Website: www.lymphoedema.org/lsn

Other useful links:

LE&RN: www.lymphaticnetwork.org
Footwork: www.podo.org
Mossy Foot UK: www.mossyfootuk.com

Acknowledgements and Credits

Professor Peter Mortimer and Gemma Levine are indebted to the contributors to this book who have provided research, worldwide knowledge of the condition, awareness and hope, now and for the future:

Kathy Bates, Jon Bowskill, Lynn Finch, Dr Claire Fuller, Professor Dominic Furniss, Juergen Gold, Dr Catherine Hood, Marie-Clare Johnson, Sue Lawrance, Professor James Levine, Paul J. Matts, Professor Kefah Mokbel, Dr Jonathan Moore, Rani Nagarajah, Dr S. R. Narahari, Mark Pearson, Carmel Phelan, Alex Ramsden, William Repicci, Dr Kerry Sherman, Professor Justin Stebbing, Dr Miriam Stoppard, Nigel Tewkesbury, Jane Wigg, Sue Wilkinson, and the patients who have voiced their own experiences. This publication could not have been possible without their input.

We are also immensely grateful to Her Royal Highness Princess Alexandra, the Hon. Lady Ogilvy, KG, GCVO, for providing the Foreword to our book. The Princess has worked tirelessly on behalf of many charities, but is particularly known for her work on behalf of the blind. One aspect of her work as President of Sightsavers has been supporting neglected tropical diseases (NTDs) such as river blindness and trachoma, but also lymphoedema in the form of elephantiasis. Her commitment to these common, but overlooked, diseases is extremely valued.

*

Peter and Gemma wish to thank Juzo, the compression garment manufacturer in Germany, for generously sponsoring this book. In particular, gratitude to the enthusiastic Adam Withey (sales director), who accompanied Gemma to the factory in Munich, where she met Annerose Zorn (owner) and Juergen Gold (director).

*

Gemma would also like to thank Apple:

My immeasurable thanks extend to Mr Phil Schiller, Mr David Shoebottom and Miss Laura Bonney of Apple, the American multinational technology company.

When I first started *Let's Talk Lymphoedema*, I wrote a letter to Mr Philip Schiller, the vice president of worldwide marketing at Apple Inc. (USA), who instantly put me in touch with Mr David Shoebottom, the product marketing manager in the UK.

I am indebted to Apple for assisting me, advising me and encouraging me to work on this publication. With lymphoedema in my right arm, I am now unable to use my existing heavy cameras which I have used throughout my fifty-year-long career as a professional photographer. The excellent cameras on iPad Air 2 and iPhone 6s have enabled me to continue my work. The iPad is a reliable and professional product that I can lift without any difficulty, and all of the photographs in this publication have been taken using only Apple products.

*

Peter and Gemma would also like to extend their thanks and appreciation to the following people, who have shown interest in this publication and have devoted their time to developing this project:

Dr Guruprasad Aggithaya, Carole Bamford, Philippe Bernard, Michael and Evelyne Bernstein, Peter Chadlington, Paul Ellis (LOC), Lynn Finch, Robert Freidenrich (Bio Compression Systems, Inc.), Melissa Hamnett (Victoria & Albert Museum), Abby Hignell, Andrew Jackson (Bowskill Clinic), Dr S. Kar, Terry Maher, Moore Capital Management, Penny Mortimer, Rosie Northampton, Marcella O'Brian, Richard Paxman, Antonio Scialo, Pat Kerr Tigret, Pip Tomson, Waitrose John Lewis Oxford Street.

And with additional thanks and gratitude to the following distinguished personalities, who have graciously endorsed this book with their personal quotes:

Dame Mary Archer, Lord Paddy Ashdown, Baroness Joan Bakewell, Baroness Betty Boothroyd, Dame Joan Collins, Jack Dee, Dame Judi Dench, Lord Michael Dobbs, Nicole Farhi, Sir Alex Ferguson, Frederick Forsyth, Baron Charles Guthrie, Lord Richard Harries, Sir Karl and Lady Jenkins, Prue Leith, Joanna Lumley, Sir John Major, Sir Trevor McDonald, Piers Morgan, Sir Sterling Moss, Sir Andy Murray, Lord David Owen, The Hon. Olga Polizzi, Alex Polizzi, The Rt Hon. Michael Portillo, Sir Cliff Richard, Angela Rippon, Rabbi Lord Jonathan Sacks, John Suchet, Terry Waite, Zoe Wanamaker.

Finally, Peter and Gemma wish to extend their appreciation to their publisher Elliott & Thompson. In particular, Chairman Lorne Forsyth, outstanding and meticulous editor Jennie Condell and her brilliant team, Pippa Crane and designer Karin Fremer.

Index

A

acute dermato-lymphangio-
adenitis (ADLA) 176
Africa 180–185
AIDS 47, 54, 129, 131
see also HIV
air travel 1, 52, 62, 124, 133
Alexandra, Princess ix
Alzheimer's disease 41
amyotrophic lateral sclerosis (ALS)
47, 129
ankles 12, 20, 22, 29, 30, 39, 69,
74, 168, 198
anogenital granulomatosis (AGG)
163
antibiotics 19, 20, 22, 23, 30, 56,
59, 60, 129, 157, 162, 178,
181
Arizona State University 115
armpit 11, 34, 35, 45, 46, 62,
110, 125
arthritis 30, 57
rheumatoid 41, 188
Asia 175–180
Australia 141

Ayurvedic medicine 178–179

B

bandages 3, 57, 80–86, 113,
116, 125, 157, 178, 179
Bates, Kathy 54–55, 124–131
Belgrado, Professor 102
blood pressure 15, 29–30
Bodyflow 107
Bowskill, Jon 73–75, 189

C

cancer 3, 5, 36, 48, 51, 53, 58,
61, 67, 78, 120, 125, 128,
134–136, 163
bladder 18
breast ix, xi, xiii, 1, 34–35,
44–46, 60–63, 68, 72–73,
94, 106, 110, 125, 132,
137, 141
cervical 22, 163
chin 160
gynaecological 142, 163
head 159
lung 67

metastasis 131

neck 159

ovarian 67, 125

penis 163–165

prostate 163

salivary glands 159

throat 160

tongue 159, 160

tonsils 159

treatment 33–36, 44–46, 48,
    51–52, 61, 65, 132–134,
    142

voice box 159

see also chemotherapy;
    lumpectomy; mastecto-
    my; radiotherapy

cardiovascular disease 15, 131

cellulitis 15, 18–20, 22, 23, 36,
    37, 52, 59, 60, 70, 82, 95, 97,
    124, 129, 157, 168, 171, 172,
    176, 179

chemotherapy 1, 35, 45, 62, 65,
    72, 94, 110, 132

taxanes 35

cholesterol 15

compression 79–95

    alternatives 102–104

    garments 4, 20, 22, 23,
        56–57, 62–64, 70, 78–80,
        85–95, 98, 102, 110, 111,
        113, 123, 129, 133, 135,
        138, 141–143, 149, 157,
        164, 173, 182

pumps 2, 104–105

    see also bandages

Cotswolds 56

Crohn's disease 163

D

decongestive lymphatic therapy
    (DLT) 85–86

Deep Oscillation therapy 106

deep vein thrombosis (DVT) 27,
    38, 55, 59, 87

Derby 42

Detlefsen, Emma 131

diabetes 187, 197

diuretics 56, 57, 69

E

electro-therapy 106

elephantiasis 14, 18, 37–38,
    175–185

    see also filariasis *and* podo-
        coniosis

elevation 39, 56, 69

Ellis, Professor Paul 3

Ethiopia xii, 180, 181

exercises 189–195

F

fat 23, 32, 113, 116, 120,
    166–167, 170–172, 197

    see also obesity

feet xi, 12, 26, 96–100, 153, 154,
    155–156, 157, 159

filariasis xi, 37–38, 44, 51, 174
    Global Programme to Elimi-
        nate Lymphatic Filariasis
        (GPEF) 179
    lymphatic or elephantiasis
        175–178, 180
    podoconiosis (non-filarial
        elephantiasis) 180–185
Finch, Lynn 80–81, 84–85
Fluoroscopy Guided Manual
    Lymphatic Drainage (FG-
    MLD) 102
Fuller, Dr Claire 180–185
Furniss, Professor Dominic
    65–66, 108–114

G
genetics 25–28, 40, 43, 46, 145,
    156, 167, 180
Germany 4, 91
Glasgow 115
Global Programme to Eliminate
    Lymphatic Filariasis (GPEF)
    179
Gold, Juergen 90–94

H
heart:
    disease 12, 67
    failure 57
    rate 74
Hinds, Pearl-Ann 130
HIV 17, 41
    see also AIDS

Hood, Catherine 137–141
hydrocele 44
hydrops fetalis 145–146

I
Iker, Dr Emily 128–129
immobility 28–31, 44
    see also mobility
immune system 17–19
    auto-immune disease 131
India xii, 175–176, 179, 180
Indocyanine Green (ICG) lym-
    phography 63–65, 102
infections 17–23, 30, 31, 37, 45,
    56, 59, 60, 70, 81, 97–99,
    124, 133, 152, 155, 164, 175,
    176, 178, 181
    recurring 19–23
    see also cellulitis
insect bites 37–38, 97, 124, 133,
    175–176
Institute of Applied Dermatology
    (IAD), Kerala 175, 177, 179
International Foundation for Der-
    matology 180
intimate relationships, maintain-
    ing 137–143

J
John Radcliffe Hospital, Oxford
    xiii
Johnson, Marie-Clare 71–72
Juzo 90–94

K

Kase, Dr Kenzo 106

Kerala 175, 177, 178

kidney disease 12

Kinesiology Taping (KT) 106, 107

L

Lawrance, Sue 80–81, 84–85

Levine, Gemma xiii–xiv, 1–4, 189

Levine, Professor James 115–121

Light Emitting Diode (LED) 105

lipoedema 166–170

    genetic cause 167

    -lymphoedema syndrome
    166

liposuction 23, 113, 170

liver disease 12

London 42

London Oncology Centre (LOC)
    137

Low Level Laser Therapy (LLLT)
    105

lumpectomy 36, 94

lymph glands 6–7, 11, 12, 31, 32,
    33–36, 45, 61, 64, 112–113,
    159, 175

lymph node transfer (LNT) 112

lymph system 5–9

Lymphatic Education & Research
    Network (LE&RN) 47–48, 52,
    54, 55, 129, 130, 131, 200

lymphatico-lymphatic bypass
    (LLB) 111, 112, 113

lymphaticovenular anastomosis
    (LVA) 109–111

Lymphoedema Support Network
    99

lymphoedema:

    abdomen 22, 157

    and animals 93, 188

    and cancer 3, 44, 106, 131,
      143

    and cellulitis 18

    and genetics 21, 25–28, 43,
      46, 131, 145–146, 156,
      163, 187–188

    and obesity xi, 15, 31–32,
      44, 114, 115–121, 166,
      170

    and old age 29–30, 42

    and rosacea 161–162

    and skin care 18

    and surgery 108–114

    and water 189

    and weight 121

    ankles 59–60

    arm xi, 1, 11, 36, 46, 72–73,
      76, 125, 141–142, 152,
      153, 159, 174

    awareness and diagnosis
      47–68

    body 152

    breast 36, 76, 79, 88, 102,
      106

    causes 25–40

    children with 145–158

exercise and physical therapy 70–75

eyes 153

face 36, 79, 106, 152, 153, 159

filarial 53, 96

see also filariasis

foot xi, 12, 26, 96–100, 153, 154, 155–156, 157, 159

genitalia 12, 22, 36, 76, 79, 88, 102, 106, 157, 159, 163–166, 171

growing up with 146–157

hands 106, 147, 148–152, 153

head 12, 76, 79, 102, 159–162

how common 41–46

leg 11, 12, 20, 22, 28, 36, 42, 59–60, 131, 152, 153, 157, 171, 174

living with 123–143

measuring 102, 103

neck 12, 36, 76, 79, 102, 159–162

new and alternative treatments 101–114

of the gut 168–174

primary 25, 43, 44, 53

risk factors 45–46

screening and early diagnosis 60–66

secondary 25, 53, 65, 108

standard treatments 69–100

torso 76, 79, 88, 159

worldwide 175–185

lymphoscintigraphy 64–65

M

manual lymph drainage (MLD) 75–77, 85–86, 102, 105, 132, 157, 160

Marr, Rikki 195

massage 75–77, 94, 139, 143, 147, 164, 178, 179

see also manual lymphatic drainage massage (MLD)

mastectomy 36, 94, 125, 220

Mayo Clinic 115

McMaster, Philip xiii

Mensedick 189

Merrick, Joseph 50

Milroy's Disease 26

mobility 95, 118, 177, 178

reduced/restricted 71, 124

see also immobility

Moffatt, Professor Christine 41–44

Mokbel, Professor Kefah 34–36, 45–46

Moore, Dr Jonathan 56–59, 66

Mortimer, Professor Peter xiii–xiv, 3, 4

Mossy Foot Clinic 181, 184

multiple sclerosis 41, 47, 129, 188

Murray, Andy 5
muscular dystrophy 47, 129

N
Nagarajah, Rani 32, 171–173,
     197–199
Narahari, Dr S. R. 175–180
National Institutes of Health (NIH)
     50, 131
Nazeer, Dr S. 2
neglected tropical diseases
     (NTDs) ix, 38, 175, 180
New York 47
nutrition 197–199

O
obesity xi, 15, 31–32, 44,
     114–121, 166, 170
          see also fat
Oxford Lymphoedema Practice
     65, 108, 110

P
Parkinson's 47, 129
Pearson, Mark 76–79
Perometer 102, 103
Phelan, Carmel 2, 61–62,
     131–134
physiotherapy 70–75, 147
PhysioTouch 106
podoconiosis (non-filarial el-
     ephantiasis) 38, 96, 175,
     180–185

pregnancy 12, 166
Proteus syndrome 50

R
Radiation Action Group Exposure
     (RAGE) 35
radiotherapy 1, 34–36, 45, 62,
     65, 72, 94, 132, 159
Ramsden, Alex 65–66, 108–114
Repicci, William 47–55, 129
Royal Marsden Hospital 3
Ryan, Professor Terence xiii

S
sentinel lymph node biopsy 34
septicaemia 18, 22, 60
Sherman, Dr Kerry 141–143
Sightsavers ix
simple lymphatic drainage (SLD)
     79
skin 1, 13–15, 18, 21, 22, 29, 36,
     37, 39, 64, 80, 81, 86, 109,
     161–162, 171, 179–183
     care 18, 157, 95–100
St George's Hospital, Tooting 3,
     78
Stebbing, Professor Justin 124
Stoppard, Dr Miriam 66–68

T
Tewkesbury, Nigel 96–100
tissue dielectric constant (TDC)
     102

trauma, accidental or surgery
32–33

U
UK ix, xii, 17, 19, 42, 101
USA xii, 2, 47–48, 50

V
varicose veins 27, 28, 38–40
    and genetic factor 40

W
weight 52, 78
    gain 45, 115
    loss 30, 32, 49, 114–121,
        129, 199
    see also fat *and* obesity
Wigg, Jane 101–107
Wilkinson, Sue 134–137
Wimbledon 150, 152
World Health Organisation
    44,175, 179

Z
Zorn, Annerose 90–94
Zorn, Julius 94